Illegal Leisure

The normalization of adolescent
recreational drug use

**Howard Parker, Judith Aldridge
and Fiona Measham**

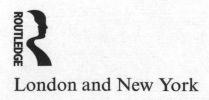

London and New York

First published 1998
by Routledge
11 New Fetter Lane, London EC4P 4EE

Simultaneously published in the USA and Canada
by Routledge
29 West 35th Street, New York, NY 10001

Typeset in Times by Routledge
Printed and bound in Great Britain by Clays Ltd, St Ives PLC

British Library Cataloguing in Publication Data
A catalogue record for this book is available from the British Library

Library of Congress Cataloguing in Publication Data
Parker, Howard J.
    Illegal leisure: the normalization of adolescent recreational drug
    use/Howard Parker, Judith Aldridge, and Fiona Measham
    Includes bibliographical references and index
    1. Teenagers Drug use Great Britain. 2. Drug abuse
    Great Britain. 3. Risk-taking (Psychology) in adolescence Great
    Britain.
    I. Aldrige, Judith. II. Measham, Fiona. III. Title. IV. Series.
HV5824.Y68P346 1998
98 10388
362.29'12'0941   dc21
                                                   CIP

ISBN 0–415–15809–5 (hbk)
ISBN 0–415–15810–9 (pbk)

Contents

Illustrations

Tables

Figures

Acknowledgements

We inevitably have a very large number of people to thank for their support and help over the past five years. Most of all we must thank over a thousand young people who took part in this study and the hundreds who actually stuck with us for five years. Thanks also to the schools which worked with us in the earliest part of the study. Special thanks to: Peter Ainsworth, Kevin Brain, Jon Breeze, Chris Carey, Gemma Cox, Sarah Curruthers, Forrest Frankovitch, Bernard Gallagher, Kathleen Kendall, Dominic MacKenzie, Russell Newcombe, Anne Pearcey, Craig Ruckledge, Eddie Scouller, Jon Shorrock, Julie Trickey and Paul Wilding.

We are very grateful to Dianne Moss for providing unstinting administrative and secretarial support throughout the study.

Introduction

Whilst there have been several significant post-war drugs arenas, ranging from 'speeding' mods in the sixties to 'tripping' hippies during the seventies through to a new wave of heroin users during the 1980s, all these scenes involved atypical minority populations. They were essentially subcultural drugs scenes and were explained accordingly.

However, the 1990s have seen the emergence of something quite unprecedented – widespread drug use amongst very large numbers of ordinary, conventional young people. This dramatic increase in drug trying and drug use amongst young Britons who have grown up during the 1990s is primarily based around cannabis with strong support from LSD and the 'dance drugs' (poppers, amphetamines and ecstasy). Indeed so widespread has the trying and use of these drugs become and so shocked have been adults' worlds that a major media-led 'debate' has emerged making young people's drug use the most written and broadcast about youth topic of the decade. Unfortunately this 'debate' is rather more a closed discourse dominated by a particular set of ideas and beliefs about the nature of drugs and the fate of those who take them. In fact this 'war on drugs' discourse has undermined public understanding of young people's drug use by circulating misconceptions and misunderstandings. This discourse, with its indifference to accuracy and inherent fear of complexity and contradiction, has had such potency, such hegemony, that it also guides official drugs policy, certainly in respect of young people's drug use.

There is little doubt that young people's drug taking poses major dilemmas for our society. When we find that half this generation has tried an illicit drug by the end of their adolescence and perhaps a quarter are fairly regular 'recreational' drug users, we can no longer use pathologising explanations. Today's young recreational drug users are as likely to be female as male and come from all social and educational backgrounds. They cannot be written off as delinquent, street corner 'no hopers'. It is clear we need to understand this social transformation in a very different way. *Illegal Leisure* tries to do this. It is based on a unique five-year longitudinal study tracking several hundred ordinary young people whose adolescence spanned most of the decade. Through the monitoring of this sample's use of leisure time and the significance of drinking and drug taking, this study builds up a clear picture of how recreational drug use fits into young people's notions of 'time out' from the stresses and strains of growing up in an uncertain 'risky' post-modern world.

Chapter 1 reviews the research literature describing the way young people's drug use has evolved during the decade. It also documents how the war on drugs discourse has developed, before considering the theoretical crisis that youthful drug taking has created for traditional psychological and criminological perspectives of adolescent development. The obsolescence of much of this theory makes the creation of new explanations particularly challenging not least because recent theoretical developments, such as post-modernity theory, have yet to engage fully with the everyday realities of growing up into the twenty-first century.

Chapter 2 is an unusual methods chapter because it must describe five years' enquiry whereby the young subjects of this study were tracked from when they were 14 years old in 1991 through until their entry into young adulthood. Using annual self-completion questionnaires and some interviews when the respondents were around 17 years old, the way this generation have 'consumed' leisure was faithfully documented. Such an ambitious investigation created many dilemmas and contingencies not normally faced by social researchers whilst also producing exciting analytic possibilities.

Chapter 3 looks at young people's favourite psycho-active drug – alcohol. It begins with an original overview of how young people's drinking has changed during the 1990s before looking at the shifting role of alcohol throughout the respondents' adolescence. Alcohol remains central to 'time out', to 'having a laugh' with friends and romantic partners. Drinking alcohol is an already normalised social activity and is central to understanding how young people extend their psycho-active, pick 'n' mix repertoire to other drugs, particularly cannabis.

Chapter 4 presents an overview of the extent to which the young people in the North-West Longitudinal Study have become involved in illicit and illegal drug use during their adolescence. It shows how drugs 'offers' and trying of a range of drugs expand through adolescence and how more regular users start to be identifiable. It also describes the self-reported positive and negative outcomes of drug use.

Chapter 5 reaps the benefits of a longitudinal study by describing the drugs pathways young people take through time. It shows how, whilst a significant minority have never taken drugs, others become drug triers or more regular drug users. The key message from this analysis is how dynamic and ever changing are the drug decision-making journeys adolescents make over many years, as through experience and maturity, they assess and reassess their attitudes to leisure and pleasure and the psycho-active options available.

Chapter 6 provides a descriptive analysis of these journeys using extensive quotations from the young subjects. When was their first time, how did they feel? What persuaded them not to try certain drugs but to use others? Young Britons use a cost-benefit assessment in reaching their conclusions about drug taking, but must rely very often on personal experiences and those of others transmitted via drugs 'stories'. Unlike the 'war on drugs' warriors they differentiate between the costs and risks for each different drug and have clear ideas about what distinguishes sensible drug use from chaotic or dependent drug taking.

However, clear-headed assessments and actual hedonistic behaviour are sometimes separated and we must also hear the stories of a minority of young 'problem' users and of others who sometimes made ill-considered, drink-affected, decisions about drug taking episodes for which they paid a price.

Once we have looked in detail at how young people have embraced recreational drug use during the 1990s and at how almost all, whether they take illegal drugs or not, have had to become *drugwise*, we are left with an analysis which is almost the complete antithesis of that which makes up the official 'war on drugs' assessment. The final chapter pulls together the six dimensions which make up our normalisation thesis and juxtaposes the realities of recreational drug use with current drugs policy. There is little doubt that the credibility of current legislation and policy, already badly undermined, will continue to be eroded further. Today's youth have reached some fairly clear conclusions about the role of drugs in their lives. Ironically their collective assessment is more coherent and far less partial and contradictory than that of the State.

1 Why are more young Britons taking drugs?

Competing and confusing explanations

Introduction

In this opening chapter we describe the persuasive evidence that far more young people from all social backgrounds are trying a range of illicit drugs. We also ask why we currently have no satisfactory explanations as to why this social transformation has occurred. Traditional sociological and psychological explanations of 'deviance' in adolescence are found wanting, being increasingly caught out by social change. Unfortunately in the absence of any persuasive, authoritative explanations of this widespread drug taking, lay discourses, constructed through the media, have come to dominate the debate. Fundamental to this 'war on drugs' type discourse are a number of misconceptions. 'Blaming' youth and perceiving drug taking as bad, dangerous and tied to delinquency and crime are all foundation stones of this inadequate explanation.

We must understand how this 'everyday' misconception has arisen since it currently distorts the way adults in general and politicians in particular misrepresent the nature of most young people's drug taking.

Blaming youth

The youth–drugs–crime–danger media mix

The blaming of youth for the ills of society is nothing new. Indeed it is such a well-documented and recurring activity (Cohen, 1973; Pearson, 1983; Goode andBen-Yehuda, 1994) that it probably has important social functions beyond stigmatising particular youthful behaviour. Perhaps blaming the young should be listed as a milestone whereby once uttered, 'the trouble with kids today' (Muncie,

1984) is the password which signals the pathology of a mid-life crisis.

There is little to be gained, however, from blaming adults for blaming youth. The quality and depth of public debate is largely determined by the media. The events and experiences they choose to highlight and elevate, when faced with a barrage of real events and press releases from professional opinion makers be they agents for stars, propagandists for a particular issue or whoever, are significant. This process is extremely complex and often contradictory. How the news is made and its impact on public perception is a subject in its own right (Moores, 1993).

The reason we must start a book reporting on a scientific study of young people in such a 'political' way is quite simple. The key themes in this book – *youth*, *drugs* and *crime* – are the very same topics which have dominated domestic or home affairs in Britain and Northern Ireland through the 1990s. The fourth leg of what is almost an 'official' matrix, a potent mix, which journalists use to frame any youth–crime–drugs story is *danger*.

We must go back to the 1980s to understand how this process acquired its enormous potency. The early and mid eighties saw the development of what was then an epidemic and is now an endemic, heroin-using population. Around 100,000 young adults from across the UK but notably in the Scottish cities and urban London and north-west England became involved. Most were under-qualified, unemployed and their needs neglected in a period of Thatcher-led economic and social reconstruction. That so many people from the country's poorest marginal communities became heavily involved in heroin was, at the time, regarded as an enormous social problem. Major public policy initiatives were launched and new 'ringfenced' resources were targeted at the problem. Initially the main reason for this was that a real and significant link between regular heroin use and acquisitive crime was established. By and large the criminologists, politicians and the public agreed about this. A series of 'convincing' television documentaries from *Panorama* and *World in Action* teams made the case watertight. The drugs–crime link was made (Parker *et al.*, 1988).

The heroin users, particularly the injectors, continued their notoriety with the arrival of AIDS and the evidence, particularly from Scotland, that needle sharing had infected large numbers of young adult injectors. The fear of an HIV/AIDS epidemic, partly transmitted by drug users, sustained drugs stories until the end of the decade but this time emphasising the drugs–danger or indeed drugs–death linkages.

A major public health campaign 'Heroin screws you up' was launched in the late 1980s. It portrayed the heroin user as a junkie, as dirty, sick and dangerous. The junkie lived in the shadows of stairwells in high-rise flats. He would rob you or pressure you into taking heroin and then infect you with death. Significantly this is exactly the image of heroin users that the young people in this study held in their early adolescence. They had watched this portrayal as children and it had been one of the first messages they received about drugs. It probably had more effect on them than on its intended audience of 'at risk' young adults.

The drugs–crime and drugs–danger sides of the mix were in place, having evolved from real events and real processes. There were indeed connections between heroin use and certain sorts of crime and between users' injecting practices and HIV/AIDS. These linkages were sustained and reinforced by a steady flow of stories about both ordinary and extraordinary people who died of drug misuse and/or AIDS.

For just a brief period at the end of the 1980s there was a sense that, if not slain, the dragon had at least been temporarily repelled and drugs stories fell away. Indeed there was space for the media, orchestrated by senior police officers, to create the 'lager louts' (ACPO, 1988). This time the peaceful tranquillity of English shire towns was being destroyed by drunken young men who *had* jobs and money to spend. They thus had no excuse and their behaviour, in fact borne of long tradition (Tuck, 1989), was temporarily held up as an example of modern moral decay. The towns in question have somehow survived intact!

It was still not school-aged children who figured in the next wave of concern. The media at the end of the 1980s began to run with two other matrix themes. 'Crack' stories from the USA, alongside dire warnings for Europe, of a drug with highly addictive powers leading to a trail of prostitution and drug-driven crime, ran into the new decade (Mott, 1992). That the crack stories spread far more quickly than cocaine use owes much to the power of the media. Crack stories epitomised the ideal news item since drugs-crime and danger were all present in abundance, and indeed if crack cocaine incidence had followed the earlier heroin 'spread' these stories would have been well founded (Parker and Bottomley, 1996).

The other big drugs story which snowballed into the 1990s concerned ecstasy (Henderson, 1997). Despite its extensive use socially and therapeutically in the USA during the 1980s ecstasy only reached public consciousness in the UK near the end of the decade. It was first headlined because the social context for its use, the 'rave' dance scene

Table 1.1 The media mix

Young burglers driven by £80 a day drug habit *Daily Mail*, 6 July 1992	Crack spawns Crime epidemic. *Observer*, 15 November 1992
Teenagers who take to a life of drugs and crime. *Daily Express*, 1 November 1993	What will your kids be doing tonight? Crack? Ecstasy? The story that will shock Britain. *Sunday Mirror*, 12 June 1994
Three reasons to riot: drugs, drugs and drugs. *Observer*, 18 May 1997	
LSD experiment traps two students in rape nightmare. *Daily Express*, 24 August 1993	Hooked by the Deadly Ecstasy Lie. *Daily Mail*, 31 July 1992
School drugs culture explodes as dealers offer sale or return. *Sunday Times*, 2 February 1997	Drugs fear for under 11s. *Guardian*, 31 January 1996
Schoolboy pushers locked up: on a tragic day of drugs shocks for every parent. *Daily Mail*, 19 September 1996	The pocket money drug addicts: millions of youngsters experimenting. *Sunday Express*, 19 January 1997

in the UK, was initially not just found in night-clubs but in large 'unofficial' parties held secretly in unlicensed venues such as warehouses and aerodromes. Like new age travellers and protesters, young 'ravers' were not acceptable and indeed attracted specific legislation such as the 1994 Criminal Justice and Public Order Act. It is now illegal to hold an 'unlicensed' rave and police can prevent the movement of people thought to be journeying to such an event (Smith, 1997; Measham *et al.*, 1998).

The more worrying aspect of ecstasy was its role in a series of highly publicised deaths among young 'ravers'. This added *youth* to the media mix. 'Ravers' were not from the excluded zones where long-term junkies lived. They were younger, of both sexes and from all social classes. They were often articulate and argued their case. They didn't get drunk and fight each other, they danced and hugged each other. The official reply was that ecstasy is a Class A drug, you are breaking the law, committing a crime, and ecstasy is very dangerous. At best, it will lead you into a dependent drugs career and further crime; at worst it will kill you.

The media mix becomes public policy

Over the first half of the nineties blaming youth and reducing complex social issues to simplistic soundbites went beyond media constructions. It became a device of government. It is perhaps unfair to say that this was led by the Home Office since most civil servants at least were not impressed by the policies and behaviour of Michael Howard who was Home Secretary from 1993 until 1997. He leaves a dreadful legacy in much drugs, penal and criminal justice statute and policy. His attack on youth began in the early 1990s but crystallised at the 1993 Conservative Party Conference when he castigated 12–14-year-old 'persistent offenders' for the rising crime rates and sense of insecurity (genuinely) felt by the public. The then Home Secretary had read his tabloids:

> We're all sick and tired of reading about young hooligans who've endlessly stolen cars, burgled houses and terrorised communities. We'll set up separate secure centres for 12–14-year-olds who at the moment can't be locked up at all and we must get on, pass the legislation, build these centres and take these thugs off the streets, that's what we've got to do.

The blaming and objectification of young people continued on several fronts. Each summer when public examination results for 16- and 18-year-olds were announced and standards measured by pass grades showed an improvement, the media suggested that the exams *must* be getting easier. The government response most years was to concur and call a review or enquiry into standards. On the moral front young women from poor communities were accused of getting pregnant to jump public housing waiting lists. Perhaps to discourage sexual activity another Conservative MP called for the censorship of teen magazines like *Sugar* on the grounds that they provided 'inappropriate' sexual knowledge and encouraged promiscuity.

Although happy to moralise about discipline and punishing the young, the government, through the first half of the 1990s, chose to 'ignore' all the indicators that showed that, for the first time in the UK, a range of 'recreational' drugs was becoming readily available and was being widely used amongst school-aged children, particularly those who were 14–16 years of age. The three key government departments in England, the Department of Health, the Home Office and the Department for Education and Employment, rarely spoke together about this issue and when they did it was often with acrimony, criticising each other's responses. The Department for Education during this very same period withdrew previously earmarked funds to employ school drugs co-ordination officers from local authorities. The Home Office spent large sums of money on a wasteful cosmetic approach to drugs education in Phase I of the Drugs Prevention Initiative. The Department of Health did however commission a piece of research on how to better co-ordinate responses to local drugs problems. *Across the Divide* (Department of Health, 1994) did at least prompt inter-agency co-operation, but significantly, in calling for information sharing and partnership between a wide range of professionals and agencies, it made no mention of the divide between young people and their 'professional' elders. There was to be no input from youth itself. The young were defined as objects to be changed not subjects with knowledge, views and ideas about the use of illicit drugs.

As evidence of drug use amongst the young increased and demands for action reached new heights the government decided to repackage its 'strategy'. It too followed and promoted the addition of youth to the matrix of drugs, crime and danger. To admit that a lack of co-ordination and corporate strategy was part of the drugs problem was an honourable admission and in late 1994 it was decided that the main government departments should have their political heads banged together. John Major claimed that he was the headbanger, 'the drugs menace remains and trends are worrying. Consequently, earlier this year, I ordered a comprehensive review of our domestic drugs strategy. . . . It proposes the most far-reaching action plan ever on drugs' (HMSO, 1994).

That the previously intransigent signed up to the subsequent strategy *Tackling Drugs Together*, which was, with some small differences, to apply to all the countries of the UK, counts as a major achievement. That a Conservative government should outline a new strategy demanding information sharing, clear objectives, inter-departmental co-operation, and regular monitoring, made this a directive laden with irony. Models of good practice were then, and remain, realities found only at the regional and local level. As a consequence little changed, certainly for central government relating to England, in respect of drugs policy and action until a change of government in mid 1997.

Tackling Drugs Together was important because it allowed central government to shift the responsibility for inertia from its own Whitehall world to the local level where multi-agency teams and partnerships must now wage the 'war on drugs'. The first premise was that young people are 'at risk of drug abuse' and succumb because of peer-group pressure. Secondly drugs are dangerous and a menace. Thirdly, because drug use leads to crime, local communities are themselves at risk, this time from the drug users. 'Media mix' speak had won the day. Youth now joined 'drugs–crime' and 'drugs–danger' and that was official as John Major, the then Prime Minister, made absolutely clear in announcing this strategy in a speech to the Social Market Foundation (9 September 1994). He chose 'yob culture' as the soundbite he wanted the media to headline. So *Tackling Drugs Together* was about offenders and crime indeed, 'no single crime prevention measure would be more significant than success on the front against drugs'. Drugs and crime were part of the 'yob culture'. The objective must be to 'make a real effort to build an anti-yob culture'.

In short, *Tackling Drugs Together*, whilst it did support prevention and treatment initiatives, was primarily part of what was the law and order 'two nation' rhetoric of a doomed Conservative government. This discourse was in reality led not by John Major but by Michael Howard. So potent is this approach felt to be in winning votes, hearts and minds that it was hijacked by the Labour Party in opposition and then prioritised as policy upon its election in 1997. The war-on-drugs rhetoric of government was thus maintained but by appointing a drugs Tsar to lead its anti-drugs strategy new ministers were further enabled to distance themselves from taking responsibility for a failing strategy or alternatively presenting a more controversial one.

The essential problem with current government policy on drugs in the UK is that it cannot deal with complexity. It cannot distinguish between types of drugs, types of drug users, diverse reasons for taking drugs and the fact that the drugs–crime and drugs–danger relationships are both real and illusory depending on these other factors. Cannabis may as well be heroin, a weekend amphetamine user a crazed addict, a young woman who gives a friend an ecstasy tablet a drugs baron.

The construction of public policy on such insecure foundations as a media-defined matrix has been totally inappropriate. Youth and the nature of adolescence is deliberately and purposefully misdefined. Throughout the 1990s government has ignored research evidence, civil service and judicial wisdom and, in refusing to recognise that dealing with complexity is a skill required to govern, has failed to understand youth. The Conservative administration of the 1990s took no heed of evidence produced by its own administrators, for instance that transitory 'delinquency' in adolescence can and must be managed differently from persistent long-term offending (see Graham and Bowling, 1995; Hagell and Newburn, 1996). It was no more sophisticated in presenting the country with a drugs strategy. *Tackling Drugs Together* was knee-deep in simplistic rhetoric which actually instructed resource-starved, local inter-agency partnerships to function on misconceptions. It is some consolation that many local actors recognised this and devised more realistic strategies through local Drugs Action Teams.

The political discourse has an energy of its own. It promotes public fear and anxiety about crime, drugs and youth which in turn it then uses to interfere simplistically, and with apparent public consent, in drugs and criminal justice policy and practice (Hough and Roberts, 1998). This process, because it can barely be challenged, thus spins along reinforcing itself. The UK has distinguished itself from other European administrations, for example in Germany, by politicising drugs, crime and the state of youth. So politically and electorally important is the simplistic rhetoric that a coherent, complex approach to dealing with drug use in a rational way becomes impossible to contemplate, let alone publicly announce. We will return to drugs policy in the final chapter.

How many young Britons take drugs?

There are potentially three types of data sets or associated techniques to help us answer this question: official statistics; social surveys and qualitative studies of young people's lifestyles and leisure activities. The third approach, once so widely and imaginatively used, has, for reasons to be discussed later in the chapter, become less central in respect of understanding youth.

Official statistics

Because they are produced annually official statistics are useful in identifying trends. In relation to drug use the three best official indicators are: the number of drug users known to (mainly) treatment agencies; the number of drugs-related offences known to the police and the criminal justice system and the amounts of controlled drugs seized by Customs and Excise and the police. Unfortunately in terms of identifying drug use amongst adolescents all three indicators are of limited value. The regional 'in-treatment' data bases are dominated by older, problem drug users in treatment. Thus we find substantive information about heroin, methadone, cocaine and poly drug users in their 20s or 30s but understandably far less information about very young 'recreational' drug users. Clearly there is a small number of teenage, hard (primarily heroin and methadone) drug users identified in these data bases but certainly until the late 1990s our main conclusion must be that adolescents in the UK are either *not* having significant problems with their current drugs of choice or are not being referred to or choosing to visit these heroin-dominated services (e.g. the Community Drugs Team, the Drug Dependency Clinic, etc.). This said there are worrying signs (Parker *et al.*, 1998b) that, at the time of writing, heroin is finding its way into the drug-taking repertoires of a small number of young people, particularly from poorer communities.

Drugs-related incidents reported to the police are not collated and published. Instead only those individuals cautioned and convicted under the Misuse of Drugs Act are presented. Once again these figures only identify small numbers of under 17-year-olds. However since the end of the 1980s several important trends have been set. Firstly the number of young people found guilty of drug offences in the UK has been rising steadily right into the late 1990s. Secondly the largest single group in these statistics are 17–20-year-olds. Thirdly the range of drugs leading to cautions and convictions is increasing. Whilst cannabis continues to dominate these statistics, a sustained increase in the number of offenders found in possession or supplying *dance drugs* is occurring. Most dramatic are increases in ecstasy-related offences, followed by amphetamines, with L.S.D. offences levelling off. Convictions relating to cocaine and crack cocaine began rising in the mid 1990s.

Because these annual statistics are so easily distorted by targeted enforcement, 'lucky strikes' and changes in resources dedicated to customs activity, we should be wary of highlighting anything other than long-term trends. Nevertheless it is safe to say that more drugs are being seized and as the 1990s have progressed a much greater variety of drugs has been discovered in substantial amounts. In short, cannabis and heroin have now been joined by crack, cocaine, LSD and amphetamines as regularly seized drugs. MDMA (ecstasy) seizures have increased from zero in 1988 to 300,000 doses seized in 1993, to 5.8 million in 1996. Whilst there was a change in recording procedures in 1993 this has not altered the overall unmistakable trends. The UK now 'imports' far more drugs each year but with a plethora of 'new' drugs joining the smuggling of cannabis and heroin (ISDD, 1996). The sheer climb in each of these official indicators which was first set in the late 1980s shows no sign of falling back (Barber *et al.*, 1996).

Social surveys

One of the best methods of estimating the incidence and prevalence of illicit drug use in youthful populations is the self-report, sample survey. There are limitations with this method and much debate about the relative merits of different techniques, which we will discuss further in Chapter 2.

The strength of the household surveys (e.g. British Crime Survey) which have been undertaken during the 1980s and 1990s is their socio-economic representativeness and the large samples they are able to capture. Such surveys tend to underestimate drug use rates however and particularly where young people are concerned. There are several reasons for this. Firstly, they rely on door knocking. This means that young people, even if they are in, are then expected to disclose sensitive information to strangers. The fact that under-18s must watch their parents sign a consent form on their behalf before such an interview is likely to further undermine the interviewee–respondent relationship. This said we now have a sufficient run of well-resourced, well-conducted national household surveys to allow some clear trends to be identified (e.g. Health Education Authority, 1996). For our purposes the most important issue is that when compared with similar surveys undertaken in the mid 1980s (see Newcombe *et al.*, 1994) we have a substantial increase, almost a tripling, in the number of people reporting experience of drugs (Parliamentary Office of Science and Technology, 1996) and that this upward trend seems to be sustained through the 1990s despite some clear regional differences (Ramsay and Spiller, 1997).

Overall these surveys dealing with a wide age band found that about seven in ten respondents had been in situations where drugs were on offer and between three and five in ten had ever used at least one illicit drug. Exposure to and use of drugs was found to rise sharply from the 13–16 age group but with 18–22-year-olds being most likely to have tried or used a drug. Cannabis dominated the lifetime prevalence rates recorded.

A number of other important quasi-national surveys but using confidential, self-report questionnaires completed by under 18-year-olds in schools, are worthy of note. The University of Exeter's Health Education Unit has been undertaking general health-related behaviour surveys amongst English and Scottish school-aged children since 1981. Although not strictly representative of Scotland's and England's adolescent populations the sheer scale of these school-administered surveys covering up to 30,000 school children (11–18 years) a year in over 150 schools makes this work by Balding particularly important. Between 1989 and 1994 the proportion of 15- and 16-year-olds reporting having tried any drug has more than tripled from 10 per cent to well over 30 per cent. In 1996 Balding found nearly four in ten had tried a drug by the end of compulsory schooling (Balding, 1997). Within these figures cannabis use has grown dramatically followed by increased use of amphetamines and LSD.

A UK-wide study by Miller and Plant (1996) discovered even higher rates of drug trying with over 40 per cent of a sample of nearly 8,000 15- and 16-year-olds reporting ever having tried a drug. Scotland had the highest rates. A further large, longitudinal study in two regions of northern England has replicated these rates (Aldridge *et al.*, 1998).

An equally impressive co-ordinated series of surveys of school-aged children has been undertaken in Wales during the 1990s. This allows a national picture to be constructed for a country far less densely populated and urbanised than England. The results show that during the first half of the 1990s the population of 15–16-year-olds reporting having ever tried drugs rose from 24 per cent to over 40 per cent for boys and from 20 per cent to over 40 per cent for girls. 'Past month' use climbed from 3 per cent in 1990 to around 10 per cent by 1996. Two-thirds of 15–16-year-olds have been in situations where drugs have been offered (Roberts *et al.*, 1995; 1997).

The picture in Northern Ireland is not dissimilar, with a large-scale survey conducted in 1992 and covering nearly a quarter of the province, finding that over half of a sample of 14–19-year-olds had been offered drugs and a third had tried them, with some 12 per cent being regular users (Southern Health and Social Services Board, 1993). More recently there have been clear signs of further rises whereby over four in ten young people (by age 17 years old) in Northern Ireland have tried a drug (Craig, 1997).

In completing this overview of surveys we should not forget the steady flow of local prevalence surveys carried out across Britain and Northern Ireland. Some have considerable merit in respect of their sophistication (Wright and Pearl, 1990) or stand out because they find unusually high rates of prevalence (e.g. Oakley *et al.*, 1992) in particular areas. A review of these studies is produced annually (ISDD, 1996). The important point to make here is that although the *range* of drug-taking rates documented by these studies is gradually reducing, regional and local differences clearly remain important (see Barnard *et al.*, 1996; Meikle *et al.*, 1996). In the same way the once distinctive differences in the figures between boys and girls is disappearing with young women being almost as likely to take drugs as young men

(Hammersley, 1994; Smith and Nutbeam, 1992). Social class differences are also fragmenting with middle-class adolescents increasingly likely to report drug taking (Leitner *et al.*, 1993) and rural young quickly catching up with their urban peers (Cooke *et al.*, 1997; Roberts *et al.*, 1995).

A final comment is required in respect of the use of ecstasy. As noted earlier the British (and indeed European) media's fascination with ecstasy and youth culture has focused on the steady procession of deaths related to either its use or the social context in which it is taken and the fact that up to a million tablets are consumed every week by UK youth (Parliamentary Office of Science and Technology, 1996). Yet surveys of school-aged children or certainly those under 17 years find fairly low rates of ecstasy taking. Ecstasy comes well behind cannabis, LSD and amphetamines. However once surveys extend the age band to include 18–25s we get prevalence rates rising to 15 per cent or more (Health Education Authority, 1996). This has been because ecstasy supply and use was, until the late 1990s, primarily associated with the nightclub-dance-rave scene monopolised by a broad church of 18–30s (Saunders, 1995). Once we research the actual dance floors we find high concentrations of MDMA and indeed poly drug users primarily in their twenties (Forsyth, 1995; Petridis, 1996; Release, 1997).

In summary then, despite the different research methods and patchy geographical coverage we can piece together a useful overview. Drugs availability and drug trying has increased rapidly especially amongst young people and compared with levels described in the 1980s (e.g. Bagnall, 1988) the rise is phenomenal. Drug trying now begins at around 12–14 years and incidence and prevalence increase with age into the early twenties. The range of lifetime prevalence (i.e. ever tried) is between 25 and 50 per cent by the age of 20. Since there are some 3.7 million people aged between 15 and 19 years of age in the UK, this means that somewhere between 0.9 million and 1.8 million of them will have had some experience of drugs (Parliamentary Office of Science and Technology, 1996). A decade ago a drug-involved youth population of this size would have been unthinkable. Moreover, within this, gender and class differences are falling away as is the distinction between urban and rural populations.

This said most of this current population do not use drugs on a regular basis (Ramsay and Spiller, 1997) and their drug taking is dominated by cannabis. Both in this age group and across the UK population cannabis is the most used and tried drug although incidence rates amongst the young will soon make the estimated

7 million people in the UK having tried cannabis (ISDD, 1994) appear conservative.

On the other hand, a wider range of other drugs are now both available and used in the 1990s with amphetamine, amyl nitrite 'poppers' and LSD showing the biggest gains amongst those under 18 and the incidence and prevalence of ecstasy rising steeply in the young adult population particularly via the nightclub-dance-rave scene. As yet the use of heroin and cocaine is relatively rare (Power *et al.*, 1996) in the 1990s youth population although this situation looks likely to change before the millennium.

Qualitative community studies

The third traditional instrument for investigating drug use is the qualitative or ethnographic study whereby the researcher focuses on a particular town (Plant, 1975), friendship network (Parker, 1974), occupation (Becker, 1963) or population (Young, 1971) to explore, in depth, the use of drugs and how this process evolved and is sustained. Unfortunately such studies are far less common during the 1990s despite being an ideal vehicle to both improve our understanding of young people's hidden and 'deviant' behaviour and contextualise the headline figures produced by the stream of drugs–youth surveys.

Moving towards the qualitative, we have seen a number of focus group studies of young people's views on drug use (e.g. Coffield and Gofton, 1994; Power *et al.*, 1996; Wibberley, 1997) which also point to the conclusion that drug trying is not only widely practised in adolescence but also widely accepted in a fairly matter of fact way.

More common have been qualitative studies of the dance-rave-club scene frequented by young adults and with the focus on the synergy of ecstasy, music, dancing and clubbing (Redhead, 1993; Saunders, 1995; Thornton, 1995).

Explaining adolescent drug use

We have been able, painting by numbers, to assemble a veracious picture of the prevalence of adolescent drug taking using a multitude of snapshot surveys. However few studies have moved beyond the *what* is happening question to the *why*. Why is everything changing so rapidly and dramatically? Why is this 1990s generation of adolescents using drugs in an unprecedented way? Why have all official attempts to prevent this failed? Why do young people and their elders find drug use such a difficult topic to discuss together?

Sociological perspectives

There are three important social scientific perspectives which one would expect might explain the changing nature of drug use. Firstly we must refer to the brief but vibrant and particularly British sociology of youth cultures and subcultures which developed in the late 1960s and disappeared in the mid 1980s. This critical and *appreciative* sociological approach emerged alongside and in relation to the development of deviancy theory or interactionist perspectives.

The cluster of qualitative studies (see Mungham and Pearson, 1976; Brake, 1980) which made up this literature provided tremendous insights into how generations of youth attempted collectively to resolve difficulties of identity and role through a variety of devices be it sabotaging menial work (Willis, 1977), outwitting the police (Parker, 1974) or creating symbolic style through hair, music or two-wheeled transport (Hebdige, 1979). For many years such studies were fascinated by working-class male street-corner life (Corrigan, 1979; Patrick, 1973). It was only during the 1980s that the significance of being female (Campbell, 1981; Heidensohn, 1985) or black (Pryce, 1979; Cashmore and Troyna, 1982) began to be explored. In fact this overall project was never completed and with a few minor exceptions (Gofton, 1990; Anderson *et al.*, 1991; Graeff, 1992) the enterprise has survived rather than thrived.

There were many reasons for this. Firstly, quite simply, we have an ageing cadre of sociologists who no longer feel at ease on the street but who have not been replaced by a sufficient number of new, younger human resources. Secondly, the realignment of social science disciplines has seen a fragmentation of what enterprise there currently is, thus reducing the potency of theoretical advances in understanding modern youth. Thirdly there have been eighteen years of a Conservative government antithetical to such *appreciative*, phenomenological investigation and thus implacably opposed to funding 'why' research whether concerned with the causes of crime, increased suicide amongst young men or recreational drug use.

The marginalisation of this qualitative, empirical sociology is also probably linked to the relegation of deviance theory. Whatever its shortcomings and indeed whether this perspective is dead or not (Sumner, 1994) we should recall the reasons why it emerged and in turn stimulated such interest in youth formations. The interactionist perspective (see Wilkins, 1964; Taylor *et al.*, 1973) posed critical questions about how marginalised and 'subcultural' groups were created and sustained. It brought home the point to social science in general but sociology and criminology in particular that powerful groups or institutions in any society usually supported (in democracies) by cultural beliefs, can and do label certain behaviours deviant and unacceptable. Thus being a gay man or lesbian, a prostitute, a skidrow alcoholic or a drug user were all deemed to be morally *bad*. This stigmatisation held true during the post-war period and into the 1970s. Deviancy 'theory' showed how through the power of definition, classification, persecution and prosecution certain individuals, behaviours and lifestyles could become, in the eyes of the majority, highly stigmatised. Critiques of the 'blaming youth' discourses (Cohen, 1973; Pearson, 1983) turned the tables.

Thanks to the accumulated knowledge of this earlier sociology of youth, supported by contemporary qualitative studies (e.g. Gelder and Thornton, 1997; Brain and Parker, 1997), we can appreciate that young people's behaviour, for instance around drinking, music and fashion, which may well disturb elders, is, when viewed from the inside, just normal adolescents doing the things which are for them important and functional to do.

There are, of course, within today's youth population a minority of disordered young people as there was amongst earlier generations. So that whilst deviance theorists learnt better to appreciate gay men or chanting football supporters they struggled to deal with explaining the dangerous axe- or knife-wielding robber or the street corner 'lad' who sexually assaulted young women for a 'laff'. This is clearly a weakness in the deviance perspective as critiques both from 'feminist' and 'realist' criminologies have noted. However sociology is so subject to academic whim and fashion that these shortcomings have not been appropriately rectified and compensatory knowledge from other disciplines, for instance developmental psychology, has not been utilised sufficiently by sociologists to explain the heterogeneity of youth. We, in turn, will have to struggle with this later in the book given that our young respondents see most of their drug-related behaviour as rational consumption and the responses of those adults around them as unreasonable or ill-informed.

Psychological explanations of drug abuse

In sharp contrast to the whims and schisms which make up post-war sociology, positivist psychology appears immensely durable. In respect of explaining drug use the first thing to note is that developmental psychology, particularly of the quantitative tradition, refers to drug *abuse* and sees drug taking as a sign of abnormality. The North

American literature in particular has taken this approach much further in attempting to identify 'risk factors' which make young people susceptible to abusing drugs (Hawkins *et al.*, 1992).

Having reviewed this literature in considerable detail, Davies and Farquahar (1995) conclude that psychology's search for risk and protection factors has not made a great deal of progress particularly in providing knowledge able to 'translate easily into effective prevention/education programmes' (p. 37).

This is because this type of psychology gets bogged down in the correlation–causation minefield where individuals are broken down into 'disembodied variables' (Cairns and Cairns, 1994) with 'early and persistent behaviour problems', 'aggressive behaviour', 'disorders', 'a family history of alcoholism', 'academic failure', 'low bonding to family', 'hyperactivity' and so on being identifiers for those who 'abuse' drugs.

We can in every generation, probably in every society, find a minority of 'damaged' young people with these negative attributes and experiences. Many will indeed be drug takers and often problematic users at that. The psychological risk literature cuts its teeth on comparing 'abnormal' development with the normal. Twenty years ago counting 'drug abuse' as an activity of the abnormal might have been a valid exercise but it no longer holds. From our earlier review of drug use amongst young Britons it is quite clear that 'drug abuse' is not going to be routinely correlated with hyperactivity, early peer rejection, aggression, conduct disorders and so on. That is unless we believe that most adolescents in the UK are suffering from psycho-social disorders and are reared by alcoholic parents who use drugs or that college and university students with four A-levels who routinely use drugs (AIESEC/IPSOS, 1993; Webb *et al.*, 1996) have low esteem, lacked commitment to school and are experiencing academic failure.

Fortunately within psychology and particularly amongst social scientists amenable to crossing academic disciplines we find a far more reflexive approach to lifespan developmental processes. These social scientists (e.g. Rutter, 1989; Coleman and Hendry, 1990) have reached the conclusion that much developmental psychology over-predicts disorder and 'storm and stress' visions of adolescence and has squeezed out the choice and decision making, however constrained, involved in each young person's journey to adulthood. Whilst they accept, and in Rutter's case (Rutter and Smith, 1994), often focus on psycho-social disorders, they also readily acknowledge that there is plenty of evidence that people can break out of even the most adverse personal circumstances and social environments (Coffield *et al.*, 1986).

In the same vein an important developmental and indeed public policy question is why, given that youthful deviance, particularly delinquency, is so widespread, do the vast majority of adolescents settle down into 'normal' unremarkable adulthood and citizenship. Moffit (1993) is equally critical of this risk/abnormal developmental literature, concluding that 'almost none of the contemporary theories of delinquency do a great job in explaining delinquency that begins in adolescence and ends soon after' (p. 696).

Moffit asserts that anti-social behaviour increases ten-fold in adolescence and that most young people then move into a more conformist mode leaving a small but entrenched 'life-course persistent' anti-social or delinquent group. The traditional risk literature confuses temporary 'normative, adjustive' deviance with the behaviour of a small life-course 'pathological personality' group. Moffit is in fact a quantitative psychologist who having mixed it in multivariate punch-ups in the academic journals concludes that these developmental theories 'are woefully ill informed about the phenomenology of modern teenagers from their own perspective. I fear that we cannot understand adolescence-limited delinquency without first understanding adolescents' (p. 696). This assessment is reinforced by the conclusions of a recent British study of persistent deliquency (Graham and Bowling, 1995).

In short, the dominant psychological perspectives on adolescent drug abuse developed when youthful drug use was atypical and subcultural and tended to be a pursuit of mainly delinquent and disordered young people. Certainly this literature continues to have a place in understanding how abnormal development may involve drug misuse as one feature of a cluster of 'difficult' behaviours. However it is of very little value in explaining why towards the millennium far more, indeed a majority of young people, are trying drugs and a significant minority use them fairly regularly. On the other hand there is a more reflexive school of psychologists who would interpret recreational drug use as a normative and temporary aspect of adolescence and not indicative or predictive of personal dysfunction. Whilst we will challenge the notion that recreational drug use will be left behind by 1990s adolescents as they reach young adulthood this more reflexive perspective is encouraging.

In conclusion we have no tailor-made theoretical perspective to answer the *why* questions. The once active sociology of youth and youthful deviance has fragmented. Explanations provided by quantitative criminology and developmental psychology have become increasingly obsolete. And whilst more flexible psycho-social perspectives are being created they have not, as yet, attempted to explain or situate *recreational* drug use. Moreover, if such drug use is not restricted to adolescence but becomes an endemic feature into young adulthood a further explanatory problem will arise.

Towards a new explanatory approach

We have shown that current theoretical and conceptual frameworks are unavailable and/or unable to answer adequately our *why* questions. The disciplines which would have been expected to explain such significant increases in adolescent drug use have simply been left behind by the pace of social and behavioural change. We thus face the daunting task of attempting to construct such an explanatory framework ourselves.

The competent social researcher, particularly when conducting a longitudinal study, routinely puzzles over his or her data and what it means. Thus our brief discussion in this section about aspects of post-modernity is borne of hunches and of the sociological imagination. It is this intellectual enterprise which makes empirical, social research so challenging and rewarding.

Adolescence in post-modern times

Unless we believe that the very nature of adolescence is changing, that young people today are fundamentally different from recent generations – biologically or psychologically – then we must hypothesise that the context, the conditions in which they are growing up, is changing. What could be in flux is how adolescence is experienced by today's teenagers, in that as they journey from childhood to adulthood they must navigate through genuinely new terrain which previous generations of youth did not have to negotiate. As a result their attitudes, opinions, strategic approach to coping, to calculating risk, measuring achievement, using leisure and so on, may be functionally and quantifiably different from their elders.

Fundamentally this is what the social theory component of the post-modernity debate is about. Have things changed so much and do they continue to change so much and so rapidly that old understandings and explanations no longer function adequately? Put at its simplest post-modernity is concerned with whether 'advanced' post-industrial societies such as the UK are reshaping into a new formation that is so different from that which was the UK in the 1960s and 70s, that we can usefully talk about the end of an epoch rather than the evolution and development of the same sort of social structure. This debate is unfinished and its conclusion is not required here. What is important is that this theoretical perspective is an attempt to explain and link a whole range of social, cultural and economic changes which potentially touch each citizen. Thus the fracture of traditional moral authority, the impact of international communications and transportation, the role of global markets on product and service choice, the emphasis on consumption rather than production, the changing nature of employment and unemployment, the increased pace of life and compression of 'time–space', the reshaping of class and gender relationships, the formalisation of communication between individuals and institutions are all themes being explored by modernity commentators with a view to discovering whether complex linkages and an overarching explanation can be created or is merely endlessly 'becoming'.

Currently modernity theorists are preoccupied with their own internal academic debate and the heat generated by this. However to engage with this one must learn the discourse and realise that you join a team still at first base arguing about what modernity is and whether it is *high*, *post* or *late*. Even where the literature moves toward a particular theme, in our case 'youth culture and modernity' (e.g. Fornas and Bolin, 1995; Redhead, 1993), it is hard to locate the impact of modernity on ordinary young lives beyond the dominant themes outlined above.

We are quite clear that these issues, being discussed within social theory, are crucial to understanding how the nature of being an adolescent in Western Europe is changing and why drug use is becoming a feature of modern leisure and consumption. However making these connections is another matter.

Our difficulty in testing this outline hypothesis is that the empirical data needed are only available in fragments and often have, been collected for very different purposes. This said we do have an excellent European research literature on transitions from adolescence to adulthood in relation to education, training and work (e.g. Furlong and Cartmel, 1997; Irwin, 1995) which is genuinely concerned with demonstrating how growing up in the 1990s has been shaped by rapid social change.

A more demanding journey to adulthood

It is perhaps the case that the magnitude of recent change in the social and economic conditions in which young people grow towards adulthood is under-estimated by old and young alike. For young people things are as they are, they have no alternative experience. Adults too, particularly if they do not *critically* observe adolescents around them, tend to assume their own youthful experiences remain a valid stock of knowledge that represents how things *always* are with the young. Elders thus often fail to appreciate the scale of social and economic reconstruction over the past fifteen years and its impact on the milieu in which adolescents must attempt to grow up.

Indeed so different is the process of growing up becoming that the very definition and notion of adolescence is in dispute, with some European commentators talking about *post-adolescence* (Jones, 1991) as a recognisable stage of the life cycle and a definable phase in the transition from childhood to adulthood. There is at least no dispute in the research literature, whether it be written by psychologists, sociologists, labour market or public policy analysts from all parts of Europe, that the stage between childhood and adulthood is getting both longer and more complex (Chisholm and Bergeret, 1991). This sort of analysis is important in that it provides an essential backcloth upon which to understand the subject of this book – that is how leisure and pleasure are also being redefined particularly within youth formations.

We must begin by recognising that the labour market has changed radically. Whilst they are not alone in experiencing major changes in employment and work patterns, young people now grow up in a society where the security of a 'trade' through apprenticeship (Ryan, 1991) or the learning of a set of skills to guarantee a job for life no longer exist. Moreover with the decline of regional manufacturing industries the pool of semi-skilled and unskilled jobs has also shrunk leaving the least qualified with few prospects beyond poorly paid manual jobs in the new service industries.

Instead the majority of young people now stay on at school after 16 or engage in further education or modular, vocational training, supplementing any financial support from parents with temporary and part-time work primarily in the retail and service sectors. And where once higher education was the preserve of the few, no less than 30 per cent now enter universities and colleges, with the proportion likely to rise further.

The expansion of higher education alongside the virtual disappearance of the youth labour market, when combined with the removal of State benefits for unemployed young people under 18 and the demise of maintenance grants and introduction of tuition fees for those in higher education, produce a new montage of consequences. Firstly we have an increased delay before the vast majority of 'adolescents' achieve financial and domestic independence. For middle-class young people this dependence on family for financial support extends not just through but beyond undergraduate life (Jones, 1991). For 'working-class' young people, or those living at home, generating some kind of income reciprocity, including the sharing of living costs, kicks in much earlier (Evans and Furlong, 1996).

Overall at 18–19 years only 20 per cent of young people are likely to be financially independent. Even at the age of 24–25 years old only half have achieved economic autonomy. Whilst being female and 'working class' tend to predict earlier independence, the overall picture is of young people now not achieving financial independence until well into their twenties.

Setting up an independent home is clearly directly related to this economic status. Indeed where a decade ago about 75 per cent (Jones, 1991) of 14–19-year-olds would still be living in the parental home, more recent surveys suggest this is over 90 per cent in the 1990s. One recent large-scale survey of young people found that even by the age of 20 over 70 per cent of males and 60 per cent of females were still living at home (Graham and Bowling, 1995). In England towards the millennium it is not until their mid twenties that the majority of young people have 'permanently' left the parental home.

Even at this stage old continuities are challenged by new changes. Increasingly young adults move not into marriage and parenthood but into another transitory set of living arrangements such as the same-age household or, even if 'living with' someone, they co-habit and accept that this arrangement may not be permanent. Young women are, in turn, delaying having their first child or, increasingly, not having any children at all. In short, changes in the labour market and in education and training have extended the period when most young people are at least partly dependent on their families either financially, 'domestically' or both. Nor is their first move likely to be into a marital home. On the other hand these realignments mean that 'post-adolescents' also have fewer responsibilities, less reason to stay in and in truth more reason to go out. They, in the main, become husbands and fathers, wives and mothers far later. They do not necessarily have the rent or mortgage to pay or the garden to tend. Whilst there will be great variation in the amount of money they have to spend they increasingly share a type of leisure time. In the modern world of consumption, if you are shrewd, being male or female, ordinary or posh, heterosexual or gay, black or white does not disqualify you from being out and going out – taking *time out*. Time out as we shall see is of crucial importance to locating the meaning of recreational drug use.

The 'transitions' literature in describing this changing world readily identifies that it involves each young person in taking risks and indeed accepting that risk taking is a regular, almost routine, activity. The outcome of all this is greater variability, diversity and uncertainty for young people whereby they experience *individualisation*: that is their life course and who they journey with, what they do and where they go is less deeply etched by tradition or privilege, by gender or by social class or by growing up in a 'community' be it steel town or coal mining village, than in the past (Roberts *et al.*, 1994).

Indeed individualisation now underpins how young people are taught and trained to navigate and negotiate uncertainty. They formalise their biographies into portfolios and wear their qualifications, assessed competencies and experiences, like war medals as they march for jobs in short supply and great demand. That most young people rate successful careers as a key goal whilst simultaneously worrying or doubting they will achieve their target is symptomatic of this (Balding, 1997). However not all young people are equipped to navigate through these modern times. We must note that since economic and educational inequalities remain, choice is not evenly spread. Thus we also have a proportion of young people who have become marginalised and excluded (Wilkinson, 1995). Often their pathways have been mapped for them as they have grown up in care or done little more than survive in abusive or unsupportive family settings. They are, to return to an earlier theme, those who are noticed when public debate turns to runaways, homelessness, teenage pregnancy, crime and chaotic 'drug abuse'. These same small cohorts, found in each generation and for many reasons, do not quickly settle into conformity and citizenship. From a care-and-control perspective they are indeed problematic (Graham and Bowling, 1995). These are, for instance, the very 'at risk' groups which may well engage in serious, dependent drug use.

These changes in the routes and journey times in the transitions to adulthood although occurring differently in each country are now evident in most of Europe. There is little doubt that the trajectories of young Europeans are becoming more diverse, uncertain and for some more problematic. In Denmark the problems of and with youth are high on the political agenda. Germany in particular appears perplexed by difficulties in these transitions right across the social spectrum from those who compete for academic success, and prized apprenticeships, through to disenchanted and disengaged minorities who continue to find succour on the political and ideological fringes. Yet in other European states, such as Luxembourg, young people still seem more sheltered from the uncertainties of modern times (Chisholm and Bergeret, 1991).

The demise of youth culture and subcultures?

There is a debate within both the transitions and social change litera-tures as to whether, in the reconstruction of modern societies, youth culture itself is still a recognisable entity. This is an important issue for our enterprise because drug use, certainly in everyday explanations, is still associated with rebelliousness and deliberate rule breaking and social deprivation. Common sense at the bus stop insists they do it because they're young, *because* it's illegal and because they've not been brought up properly.

Certainly in the post-war period when the potency of Britain's class system was still overtly in place, social scientists also explained minor crime, deviance and subcultural formations such as the teddy boys, mods and rockers and even punks in this way. Similarly in working-class delinquent worlds where recreational drug taking was being established it was the distinctiveness, and the antithetical resistant nature of these formations which were emphasised (Hall and Jefferson, 1976).

Perhaps in retrospect we can now see these subcultural arenas as far more functional within the working-class male lives which were explored. Notions of masculinity and camaraderie so prevalent at the time often stoked these apparent subcultural engines. And the milder middle-class 'studenty' version of all this was indeed seen as part of youthful distinctiveness, style and statement (Young, 1971).

It is the fracturing of such subcultural or differentiated youth scenes which lends weight to those who argue that youth subculture(s) are disappearing. Post-modernist explanations of this emphasise that with *individualisation* and destandardisation and with the diversification of fashion and musical style across wide age bands it is no longer possible to identify specific youth cultural style. The development of fashion items for children, the wide range of alternative styles in the adolescent and young adult worlds, whereby there is no official 'rebellious' uniform, no standardisation by gender or class to distinguish the 15-year-old from the 25-year-old, are all held up as evidence of this reconstruction.

The role of fashion and leisure is of course all part of the centrality of consumption which underpins the post-modernist's explanation of social change. This too fits with the issues of drugs availability and the increasingly wide range of different illicit drugs used by young people. It also fits with the way the excluded groups of adolescents and young adults in the UK currently behave. As we have been at pains to point out throughout this chapter we still have consecutive generations of 'working class' or unemployed young men and women who live at the margins. Despite the success of *Trainspotting*, Irvine Welsh's book, play and film of inner-city drug use, in exposing a twilight drug-driven criminal world, today's excluded groups actively shun publicity. For them the avoidance of public scrutiny is all important as they live in the shadows, with collars up and designer hats pulled down. This is because anonymity and avoiding surveillance is a functional necessity. For those 'grafting' in the illicit economy the main goal is to raise funds to allow a transformation into being straight consumers. The reward for living in shadows, dodging the cameras and police cars is periodically to present oneself in the legitimate world of the 'match', pub and club, in the latest clothes and be seen getting the right buzz from whatever designer drinks or drugs are your pleasure. That very recent studies of these young adult criminal careers indicate that these are the main motivations of a shady, criminal life suggest that conspicuous consumption in the mainstream offers more potential theoretical power than notions of subcultural rebelliousness (Collison, 1996; Parker, 1996; Mukhtar, 1997). Traditional masculinities, incidentally, remain alive and well in such populations but nevertheless rationalist and social-control theories of crime seem increasingly useful.

Young women from the margins also struggle on and whilst modern times are treating them better in terms of educational success and an improved supply of flexible though insecure semi-skilled jobs, they still are the most likely of their female peers to leave the parental or care home not for a professional career but to be a young single mother living in poor housing and struggling on State benefits and without supportive male partners (Oakley, 1996; Carlen, 1996).

Although we lack sustained research into these issues and processes there are few contra-indicators. It does look as though any explanations of changes in young people's attitudes and behaviour are more likely to evolve from aspects of social theory found in the post-modernity debate and less likely to be found in older social class or unmodified subcultural explanations.

Indeed right across the social spectrum of youth in the UK attitudinal research suggests that it is not differential or rebellious attitudes and beliefs which motivate youthful deviance. Whilst sceptical about the political process and distrusting of the social and criminal justice systems in their countries (McNeish, 1996), British children and young people, when asked, disclose conservative and conventional social attitudes (Roberts and Sachdev, 1996) and do indeed see conventional 'successful' adulthood as a key goal. If anything these 1990s views are more conservative than those recorded for earlier generations.

In summary, therefore, whilst the post-modernity, theoretical debate is unfinished it does look as though we need to situate more specific theories of adolescence and changes in young people's behaviour within it. There is the very real possibility that 1990s adolescents are a vanguard generation. They must negotiate a new set of rules and expectations, new cultural pressures, new pathways to 'identity' and adulthood. Whether the notions of *individualisation* and *destandardisation* are consistent with *tribalism* (Maffesoli, 1995) remains unclear. What we can be clear about is that those processes which modernity commentators have emphasised do fit with how young people are experiencing adolescence and the more uncertain, extended journey to adulthood. In particular, commentaries which note that changing patterns of consumption are related to the fragmentation of subcultural worlds and perhaps even the reframing of youth culture also look promising. The challenging prediction offered is that given the potency of global fashion, leisure and 'pleasure' markets we are moving to a situation where the world of leisure is not a vehicle for transporting or displaying youthful identity but is the cultural milieu in which young people actually create their personal and social identities (Hollands, 1995).

As seductive as these observations of social change are we must not forget the old adage 'continuity and change'. A great deal remains largely unchanged. The most fundamental continuity is surely that the essential *nature* of adolescence (Coleman and Hendry, 1990) remains unchanged. Young people still aspire to grow up. They still want to be adults to create personal and social identity, to have sexual and romantic partners, to assert their independence, to take risks, to be a successful member of the age group they mix with, to experience bonding, to have a 'good job', money, success and happiness. There is no reason to believe that theories of adolescence, particularly those which have been created from a multi-disciplinary base and have acknowledged reflexivity in this stage of the life course, are becoming obsolete. It is not the nature of being an adolescent that has changed as much as the society, the context in which the young must, at best, negotiate and, at worst, realise they have very few options.

Conclusion

There is no doubt that the incidence and prevalence of drug use amongst young people in the UK, right across the 14–25 age bracket, has risen dramatically during the 1990s. We have shown that all the official indicators, such as seizures and prosecutions, have climbed continuously. National household surveys have recorded steep increases in self-reported drug use. The more sensitive, targeted, confidential surveys of youth populations, both national and regional, have concluded similarly. The UK, along with perhaps the Netherlands, Italy and Spain, is experiencing what may turn out to be a social transformation in respect of recreational drug use, which will in time affect most other European states.

In the UK, in particular, common-sense explanations of all this have been badly tainted by a strong tendency amongst politicians and the tabloid media to blame youth – to associate drug use with 'badness' and weakness. Thus recreational drug use has become inappropriately entangled in a whole set of politically 'hot' issues such as juvenile crime, falling educational standards, poor parenting and the disintegration of the traditional family, community safety and so on.

At the same time and because adult worlds are genuinely fearful, because of images of chaotic, dependent, hard drug users, as to how drug taking might damage young people, the shrill voices of blame and condemnation are mediated by calls to protect the young from the *risks* of drug 'abuse', from the harmful effects of drugs and the road to dependency and despair. Either way this continuous focus on young people's drug taking makes this the single most talked about, written and broadcast about item in contemporary discourses about the state of the young in the UK.

In many ways this public debate, trading in sound bites and over-simplifications, makes it even harder to unpack the key issues. From our perspective we have to explain how an illegal activity, recreational drug use, has spread into mainstream youth pursuits whereby youth culture has accommodated a drugs culture. What are we to make of this process whereby cannabis and dance drug use has pierced the traditional protective boundaries of being female, being middle class or living in a rural environment? We must also ask whether this is all a temporary social phenomenon or whether, instead, we are seeing the beginning of a sustained aspect of emergent new lifestyles.

When we turn to the social sciences and contemporary empirical and theoretical projects in sociology, psychology and social policy to help us understand better how this situation has arisen we are soon disappointed. Quantitative criminology and developmental psychology, still dominated by a positivist approach to correlating risk factors associated with disorder and dysfunction in adolescence, have been left behind by the pace of change in drug use – unless we believe that half this generation of young people are prone to psycho-social disorders. Moreover whilst we are handicapped by the fragmentation of the qualitative research tradition, it is also quite clear that drug use is no longer confined to subcultural worlds whether they were constructed by working-class males or alternative 'hippy' lifestyles. These drug-specific explanatory literatures which were created in the past when drug use was a more restrictive activity, now struggle to function in explaining a widespread recreational scene. With these earlier explanations now so moribund we are obliged to turn to more general perspectives on adolescence and social change when searching for broader explanatory foci or perhaps theoretical ideas to test out. In fact these more generalist perspectives look promising.

Firstly the more recent theoretical approaches to adolescence as part of the lifespan literature seem more able to cope with change because they have become far more dynamic and have broadened their perspectives by becoming multi-disciplinary, increasingly acknowledging the inter-relationship between the individual adolescent and his or her social world. This approach insists that most (but not all) young people successfully negotiate adolescence, taking 'storm and stress' in their stride. It is able to accommodate substantive changes in behavioural patterns – such as earlier sexual behaviour or later marrying – without having to pathologise or redraw the boundaries between normal and abnormal development. We can speculate that this recent life-course transitions perspective will in time explore 'recreational' drug use without schism. It implicitly reminds us that it is not the essential *nature* of adolescence which is changing but the nature of the terrain and journeys which youth must make and consequently the type of strategies and skills they utilise.

These conclusions are not inconsistent with a second pertinent literature created by a group of empirical sociologists who have been purposefully looking at contemporary transitions from adolescence to adulthood across Europe. In turn it is no coincidence that these social scientists have been deeply influenced by the post-modernity literature. They set us a good example by taking up theoretical ideas and then operationalising them through empirical research. Their conclusions are unequivocal. Being 1990s adolescents involves young people in a more difficult, more demanding and far longer journey in which coping with uncertainty about the future and the pay-offs of everyday decisions all conspire to make this a vanguard generation who must grow up in a risk society (Beck, 1992). They take risks not as an expression of rebelliousness but as a tactic to achieving conventional goals. Clearly, taking calculated risks is very different from being 'at risk'.

The post-modernity literature, despite its impenetrability and abstraction, simply has too much potential relevance to ignore. Each of the main themes in the modernity debate appear to connect to the drugs story we are about to tell. The new widespread availability of a whole range of drugs packaged and marketed for the 1990s mimics the processes of commodification and global trading and consumption patterns identified in contemporary social theory. The way in which drug use has interwoven itself into fashion, music, dancing, partying and indeed drinking, right across Europe, corresponds with theoretical ideas about global markets, the ascendency of consumption and the transportability and transnationalisation of youth culture.

We will explore these and many other parsimonious connections as we report on a five-year longitudinal study of several hundred young Britons whose adolescence has spanned the 1990s. By being able to describe and monitor how this cohort's attitudes and behaviour have developed since they were 14 we are in a good position to explore the 'why' questions as we simultaneously explore the 'what' or 'which' journeys they take.

Finally as the subtitle of this book suggests we have found the, borrowed, concept of normalisation a useful device in helping us explain the extensive growth in availability, experimentation, use and acceptability of illicit drugs by today's youth. The concept also helps us understand the reluctant acknowledgement of this situation by abstainers. We will return to this theme in the final chapter when we lay out our conclusions about whether 'recreational' drug use is in the process of becoming normalised amongst British youth.

2 The North-West Longitudinal Study

Overview

In this chapter we describe, wherever possible in a non-technical way, how we created a sample of over 700 14-year-olds (in 1991) and tracked most of them annually for up to five years. Each year we enquired about their personal and family circumstances, their disposable income, use of leisure and perspectives on personal and social relationships. We asked them in detail about their tobacco, alcohol and illicit drug use. As they matured we felt able to pursue more complex issues with them including their attitudes towards drug use and drug users, their assessment of the health education they received, and their experiences at parties and nightclubs. For those who took drugs we felt able, as they reached young adulthood, to ask them to describe their motivations for their use of individual drugs and what they experienced in so doing. We took equal care to explore the perspectives of those who had not and will not take drugs.

Five annual self-report surveys were undertaken, and eighty-six interviews were conducted when respondents were 17 years old. In the subsequent year a number of case studies of 'critical incidents' relating to respondents' own or others' drug use were explored (see Table 2.1). We begin this chapter by describing how this programme of research was financed and some of the things we learned in conducting the five-year study that researchers rarely have the opportunity to discuss. We explain how our samples were created and how the 'cohort' of respondents with complete data for five years was affected by attrition (the loss of research subjects over the years). We then describe the self-report questionnaire surveys. From there we discuss the way we set about interviewing a selected group of respondents in depth. Issues of validity and reliability are discussed but in an unusual way: because the research is longitudinal, it posed dilemmas not faced with one-off cross-sectional surveys, yet also unexpected opportunities to consider veracity more comprehensively. Finally, we describe how a 'pathways' analysis developed around Year 4 and how we set about systematically documenting the ways that our young respondents took distinctive pathways and journeys in respect of their attitudes to and use of illicit drugs.

Appropriate resources

Social research methods textbooks routinely implore investigators to combine quantitative and qualitative methods. Many sing the praises of longitudinal studies as, in the fullness of time, offering exceptional analytic power. What the textbooks and research training courses rarely consider seriously is just how expensive such studies are. The North-West Longitudinal Study was initially funded for three years by the Alcohol Education and Research Council, with the Economic and Social Research Council awarding funds for its fourth and fifth years. We also had an additional grant from the Home Office Drugs Prevention Initiative and some sponsorship from a commercial interest which paid for incentives (music vouchers) for the participants. The total cost of this was some £380,000. Put quite simply then, the main reason why this is the only contemporary longitudinal study of how young Britons' alcohol and drug use develops during adolescence is resources. It is extremely difficult to persuade funders to commit their limited resources to such expensive projects that must be funded for more than a couple of years. The trend towards more focused, one-off cross-sectional investigations which are relatively inexpensive, or alternatively household surveys in which a wide range of exploitable data can be collected has grown during the 1990s. Thus the biggest single

Table 2.1 Overview of the investigation

	Year 1	Year 2	Year 3	Year 4	Year 5
Mean age of participants	14 years	15 years	16 years	17 years	18 years
Questionnaire administered	In 8 schools	In 8 schools	In 3 schools and by post	In 3 schools and by post	All postal
Interviews	-	-	-	86	-
Case studies	-	-	-	-	8

obstacle to undertaking a longitudinal study is identifying and obtaining sufficient resources. Obtaining research awards in turn involves an often-mysterious combination of a stable research base, a good track record, a well-worked idea, timeliness and a hefty slab of luck.

We noted in the last chapter how politicised the issues of youth, drug use and law breaking have become during the 1990s. The politicised nature of the subject not only affected how we chose to fund the research, but also affected the implications of our choice of funding bodies upon how we have been able to report our findings. This project was funded by two Research Councils – the Alcohol Education Research Council (AERC) and the Economic and Social Research Council (ESRC). Research Councils normally receive their moneys directly from government and, to a certain extent therefore, this inevitably occurs within a political context of them constructing 'government friendly' mission statements, having government-selected chairs, and being accountable to government in terms of their 'successes' in forming public policy, making scientific discoveries, and funding students who successfully complete Ph.D.s. And yet, unlike government departments or private enterprise, both of which sometimes fund academic research, Research Councils remain relatively autonomous organisations. Even within a political context in which Research Councils operate, their purpose is to fund academic research judged solely within the relatively impartial sphere of academic peer review. Thus, each application for funding to a Research Council is sent out to other qualified academics working in the area who are asked to assess the application on its academic merits.

Although obtaining awards from Research Councils involves structuring lengthy, academically rigorous applications that meet 'political' funding criteria or 'themes', once obtained, the money is 'clean'. The Councils expect the project to be open to scrutiny and demand that all its results reach the public domain. Had this programme been funded by government departments this particular book would not have been written because the results would have been sanitised, or, in the face of resistance, delayed interminably by suspicious and nervous civil servants dedicated to not embarrassing government ministers. The war on drugs rhetoric and nature of 'media' politics would not have allowed the story we tell to be narrated via a programme funded by government. It is important therefore that any investigation which claims to tell it 'how it is' about such politically sensitive topics as young people's drug use should think carefully about the implications of obtaining funds from any particular source.

In relation to human resources, it has been very important that we have had a stable research team who have been committed to both completing the study and to the dissemination of research findings. The latter process has gone on well beyond the five years during which the project took place, and will no doubt continue to do so. Five years is a long time in anyone's research career and the investigation has benefited greatly from having had a stable core team throughout with only one early change in staffing. This has allowed a creativity to develop whereby innovations and 'experimental' and flexible approaches have flowed easily between team members who understand one another's strengths and interests.

'Experiencing' the research process

There are many things we have learned about carrying out such a large and complex piece of research that researchers rarely have the opportunity to write about, including the development of some important research skills not usually discussed in method texts.

The amount of information we compiled over the years was vast, and our methods for handling it evolved in response to our changing needs. For example, in the early years of the research we did not need or want to keep identifying information about respondents such as names or addresses, though in later years we needed to develop methods for collating this information that was accurate, efficient and accessible, yet also ethical. Methods for handling data also evolved in response to changing technology within the university setting. For example, in the fourth year of the research we moved to new premises in which all staff in our department were provided with powerful networked PCs with up-to-date software which we were no longer required to purchase ourselves from project funds.

In total, we tracked 1,125 unique individuals for one or more years, coded and processed 3,116 questionnaire returns, and now have available over 2,900 questionnaire variables and 'computed' variables. The analyses began in 1991 using SPSSX (Statistical Package for the Social Sciences) on a university mainframe computer, the only one available at the time to deal with large data sets, and progressed to SPSS for Windows, run on powerful PCs we acquired over the years. Eventually the data set became so large that we could no longer save it to floppy disk, and we were required to use our university's then newly available networking facilities and our own purchased tape streamers.

Simultaneously, we set up and managed a second database that we used to keep track of our respondents after they left school to record their voluntarily given names, addresses, phone numbers, as well as tracking our attempts to stay in touch with them through follow-up letters, second (and more) follow-up letters, Christmas cards, contacts of names of friends or relatives that respondents had given us in case they moved, as well as contacting respondents we had lost after Year 3 in a large door-to-door 'recapture' of lost respondents we did over one summer. The first version of this data base was initially kept by hand when the information we needed to keep about respondents was small; in later years it was maintained through PC database software (Microsoft Access). This allowed us to combine the tasks of documenting our attempts to keep track of respondents over the years, as well as the previously separate administrative tasks of producing mailing labels, thereby halving the work involved in these related tasks.

We became quite expert at data cleaning, the process of looking through data for inconsistent responses within questionnaires or 'rogue' values. If done rigorously, data cleaning allows researchers to minimise the amount of 'error' due to miscoding or inconsistent coding, always a problem with large data sets in which teams of coders must be employed. By the end of the research we had developed a comprehensive programme of analyses which automatically identified potential candidates that may have been miscoded. We also learned through the data-cleaning process about which questions were uniformly coded by our teams of coders, and which questions tended to produce inconsistent coding or miscoding. We were able then to redesign questions in later years, therefore, not only based on how well they 'worked' with our respondents, but also to minimise coding problems. Because of the sheer size of the data sets over the years, we also had to learn how to identify appropriate temporary staff to act as questionnaire administrators and coders, to identify their always varying training needs and to meet and manage these.

The research also posed ethical dilemmas we had not predicted. One young woman's postal questionnaire in the fourth year of the research showed that she was struggling with her drug use and seemed quite unable to cope. She had included with her return a few pages of extra comments detailing her problems. She did not explicitly ask us for help, and yet it was quite apparent that she felt out of control, unable to deal with her drug use, and in need of help. Our dilemma was whether or not we should contact her; to do so was to treat her as an identifiable individual rather than as an anonymous questionnaire return – was this appropriate given that as researchers we are ostensibly uninterested in 'individuals' and only interested in 'group statistics'? After much discussion, we decided that we would contact her to offer her a listening ear and to put her in touch with services if she felt that would be useful for her. The decision turned out to be a good one; she welcomed our overture, and after meeting with her, we referred her to a carefully chosen local drug services agency. But it is entirely possible that she might have resented our intrusion, and felt her privacy invaded and our promises of confidentiality shattered. Although we already had in place a set of procedures for dealing with these kinds of problems for the 'critical incidents' part of the research, we did not anticipate encountering the problem of identifying troubled young people from their questionnaire returns. We learned therefore the need to be flexible, and the need to review our policy and procedures continuously.

The most unexpected skill we were required to develop, for which we were least well prepared and equipped, was dealing with the media. Immediately following the publication of the drug use prevalence figures amongst 14-year-olds after the first year of the research, the media interest was intense. In that week the figures were quoted on radio and television, and in local and national newspapers, and we received ten or twenty phone calls a day from journalists. While the interest died down in the ensuing weeks, it bubbled up again with the publication of *Drugs Futures* (Parker *et al.*, 1995). Inbetween the periods of intense media interest, we still received on average one phone call a week from journalists, and television and radio producers. All this meant that the more outgoing members of the team were required to develop skills in dealing with journalists, including conducting live interviews on radio and television. More than one interviewer took a frighteningly aggressive tack, seeing us as condoning drug use amongst young people and taking the opportunity to 'blame the messenger'. We learned what so many others already have: that no matter how careful you are to be clear, journalists almost inevitably misquote you. We also learned that it is easy to spend a great deal of research time in providing a basic research service for journalists eager to cover such a hot topic. In the end we had to become quite ruthless in refusing interviews and help to journalists in their research in order simply to get on with our own.

Sampling

Finite resources affected our choices of sampling techniques from the outset. The statistical ideal of the random sample was neither practical nor affordable for our research. Given that we wished to follow a sample of young people for several years it was vital to contact young people economically, and this almost inevitably means via schools and in reasonably compact geographical areas. We opted for the tried and tested schools survey procedure adopted by researchers like Wright and Pearl (1990) and Balding (1997). However, unlike Balding's survey, we decided to administer the questionnaire ourselves, without teachers present, in order to embark upon a relationship with participants both at the first administration of the survey when they could feel less worried about the possibility of being identified by teachers, and through later survey administrations where they would meet us on each occasion and be reassured through experience that their responses had not been divulged to anyone, particularly parents and teachers.

Our sample comprised eight co-educational State secondary schools in the metropolitan north-west of England, and was chosen to be as representative as possible of two of the counties therein: Merseyside and Greater Manchester. It was not possible, as with a stratified random sample, to 'structure' the sample in a proportional sense on race, class, gender and socio-economic indicators because our sampling unit was the school, rather than the pupil or respondent. In order, therefore, to choose schools in which pupils *would* be representative of the metropolitan north-west of England, we first selected a borough within each of the two metropolitan counties that was deemed to be representative of the counties that contained them, and then selected schools within them to be representative of the boroughs. A detailed discussion of these procedures, along with evidence for the schools' representativeness at both the borough and county levels, is contained in the Appendix to *Drug Futures* (Parker *et al.*, 1995). In summary, however, there is compelling evidence that the clustered, non-random sample we obtained is representative in many respects of the two boroughs containing the schools within the metropolitan counties as a whole. In particular, the sample at Year 1 reflected correct proportions of respondents drawn from middle- and working-class catchment areas, respondents from single-parent families, and respondents whose parents were in paid work. The proportion of males in the sample reflects their over-representation in the population for this age group. The proportion of non-white ethnic groups in Greater Manchester is only slightly higher than its population counterpart. We can be reasonably confident, then, that our sample at Year 1 (see Table 2.2) is fairly representative of the young people in the metropolitan north-west of England.

Table 2.3 identifies the change and attrition in the samples over the years. Two processes are at work. On the one hand we 'recruited' new respondents particularly at Year 2 when we returned to the schools.

Table 2.2 Gender, class catchment and race of respondents at Year 1 (n = 776)

	School Catchment Area			Race[b]			
	Total	Middle class	Working class	Black	Asian	White	Other
	n%	n%	n%	n%	n%	n%	n%
Female	358	204	154	1125	304	5	
(row %)	46.3	57.0	43.0	3.2	7.2	88.1	1.4
Male	415	201	214	18	32	329	5
(row %)	53.7	48.4	51.6	4.7	8.3	85.7	1.3
Total[a]	773	405	368	29	32	329	5
(col %)	100.0	52.3	47.6	4.0	7.8	86.8	1.4

Notes:
[a] Shortfall in 'Total' due to three respondents whose sex was not known
[b] Shortfall in 'Race' numbers due to forty-six respondents who did not indicate their race

Given that we surveyed whole classes, we picked up new pupils as well as those who had been absent the previous year, as we did not attempt to pursue those absent on the day of the administration (though we did begin to do this after Year 3). On the other hand the loss of numbers from our original sample at Year 1 ('attrition') was also, inevitably, on-going. Furthermore, the respondents we lost numbered disproportionately among those who reported drug trying and drinking at age 14, as well as in later years (a second, but smaller group of lost respondents were Asian Muslims who numbered disproportion-ately among drink and drug abstainers). We cannot, therefore, consider the results in years subsequent certainly to Year 2 as 'repre-sentative' of young people in the metropolitan north-west of England in the way that results in Year 1 were.

What do these changes and attrition rates in the sample mean for the findings we report? Primarily, they mean that the results cannot be seen as representative, in a straightforward manner, of young people in the metropolitan north-west of England. We have no basis, therefore, on which to assert that the drug use prevalence rates found in Year 5 reflect those that we would find if we were able to survey the entire population in the north-west from which our original sample was

Table 2.3 Change and attrition in the samples[a]

	Year 1	Year 2	Year 3	Year 4	Year 5
Total Respondents	776	752	523	536	529
One Year Only	197	129	28	8	2
Two Years Only	247	252	109	37	33
Three Years Only	92	131	146	115	117
Four Years Only	240	240	240	147	148
All Five Years	229	229	229	229	229

Note:
[a] Attrition levels were not random; the respondents we lost at each stage of the research were disproportionately working class, male, Asian, black, and not in A-level education at age 17

drawn, and thus we will make no attempt to make such a generalisation. Our purpose, however, is not to estimate population parameters. In the absence of a random sample, this is best done by collating the range of surveys undertaken in the UK, as we did in the last chapter. Instead we wish to describe the 'pathways' of drug abstinence and drug use for those in our sample whom we have retained. Moreover, in spite of the shift in the structure of the sample due to attrition, we still retain members of the groups with the heaviest losses (working class, male, Asian, Muslim, black, and not in A-level education at 17), though in smaller numbers.

Given that the research is longitudinal in design, we are interested in not only describing statistics for the samples at each year, but also in exploring both how individual respondents change over time and, retrospectively, how the early characteristics of our respondents can be seen in the light of their later drug pathways. Thus, where we carry out analyses examining how individual respondents change over the five years of the study, we present these data for only those 229 respondents in the core cohort for whom we have complete data for five years. Chapters 3 and 4 provide results for the whole samples at each year (Year 1: n = 776; Year 2: n = 752; Year 3: n = 523; Year 4: n = 536; Year 5: n = 529), but Chapter 5 presents results primarily for the core cohort with complete data (n = 229). The core cohort contains *fewer* drug users than the early annual samples.

Survey procedures

Following selection of the eight schools, meetings were held with the heads and/or liaison teachers at each school to explain the aims, methods and administration of the surveys. They were reassured that no individual schools would be identified in any publication emanating from the project, and that responses of their pupils would remain confidential and anonymous. We also promised them detailed and anonymised feedback of their pupils' responses in composite tables which they have received each year. This feedback has been delivered without incident and no school has been identified publicly at any time or 'discovered' by the local media.

Administration of the surveys occurred in the autumn, avoiding the Christmas holiday season and the potential distortion of seasonal celebrations. A teacher introduced the administrators of the questionnaire to each survey group, and then left the room. The nature of the survey was explained to the group, with particular emphasis that responses would be voluntary, confidential and anonymous. After responding to pupils' questions and concerns, the questionnaires were handed out in envelopes in which they were to be sealed by the pupil when complete. Respondents took between twenty and forty-five minutes to complete their returns. The issue of *confidentiality* cannot be over-emphasised. At 14 and 15 in particular our respondents were extremely concerned about who would see their questionnaire returns and needed constant reassurance that no third parties such as parents, teachers or police officers would have access to their answers. Comments on early returns reminded us lest we forgot. 'This had better be bloody confidential. If my Mum reads this she'll kill me' (Simon). 'I think it is rather personal but I hope it helps in your research and other people are cooperative for you. I also hope you keep your promise about it being totally confidential' (Debbie).

At the end of the first administration each respondent was asked to give their initials and date of birth on a separate sheet so that the following year's questionnaire could be given to them personally. If this was seen as too risky in terms of anonymity we asked them to use a nickname they would remember. Conformity was very high and after a little detective work the researchers were able successfully to tag almost every respondent. At the end of the second year administration we asked for pupils' written permission to obtain their names and addresses from their schools. This was explained as a chance to maintain contact with the sample, over half of whom would be sixteen and leave school in a few months time after GCSE exams. Again, compliance was high. Thereafter we made direct contact with school leavers using the correspondence address they gave. By Year 5 a full contact database for over 600 participants existed which was updated when someone moved. For postal returns an incentive (music voucher with a £10 value) scheme was introduced at Year 3. In Years 3 and 4 those who attended the three schools with sixth forms were surveyed in school time. In Year 5 all participants were contacted via the post.

The questionnaire

At the fifth administration the self-report questionnaire contained four main sections: personal characteristics, general questions about drugs, questions about the last occasion of drug use and questions about alcohol. A core of questions comprising all the main 'dependent' variables (those which we are interested in explaining and predicting – such as drug offers and drug use) have remained constant across the five years of the survey. Some questions have changed, primarily for two reasons. Firstly, by the later administrations, we had benefited enormously from respondent feedback in the previous years. Many questions had been refined in some way, resulting in improved layout, better instructions and significantly reduced proportions of missing data.

In addition to modifying questions based on feedback from respondents, we also refined and elaborated on some topics, and shortened or eliminated others. In Years 4 and 5, for example, we expanded the section on drug use, limited questions on alcohol use to core questions only, and, much to the annoyance of the respondents, removed questions from previous years on sexual experiences. In designing questions for the survey, we initially drew upon questions for which evidence of reliability and validity had been demonstrated by other researchers (e.g. Plant *et al.*, 1985; Balding, 1997), as well as including new questions for which there were fewer useful precedents. By the last two years administration of the survey, we had pioneered some innovative questions to explore areas such as subjective experiences of drug use, which we felt able to ask once the sample moved into their later teens.

The main drugs-related variables in the fifth administration of the survey included:

1   attitudes toward drug taking in general;
2   for thirteen individual listed drugs: ease of access, having been in offer situations, drugs tried (including recency and frequency measures), and future use intentions;

3   the last occasion of drug use;
4   for cannabis, LSD, amphetamines, ecstasy, and cocaine/crack:
    questions on the last occasion of use, reasons for use, experiences
    during and after, and typicality of the occasion;
5   poly drug use;
6   measures of drug-related harm.

We used four question formats within the questionnaire. The first was
of the 'tick box' variety in which categories were mutually exclusive
(i.e. only one box to be ticked), and included examples such as race (in
which respondents indicated their racial backgrounds based on categories used by the Equal Opportunities Commission), attitudinal
statements in which responses could range on a five-point scale from
'agree strongly' to 'disagree strongly', and the drug offers, use/recency
and future use intentions for the thirteen listed drugs. The second type
of question was also of the 'tick box' variety, but in which categories
of responses were not mutually exclusive; in other words, respondents
could tick as many boxes as applied. This question format was used,
for example, for respondents to indicate all drugs taken on the last
occasion of drug use, as well as for reasons, experiences during and
experiences after the last occasion of use of each of five specific drugs.
The third question format was of the fill-in-the-blank variety, and was
used for questions asking number of cigarettes smoked yesterday,
income, frequency of specific drug use within the past month, amount
spent on drugs and alcohol, and number of containers (pints, cans,
bottles, glasses etc.) of alcohol consumed on last occasion and in the
past week. The fourth and final type of question format was of the
open-ended variety, in which respondents were free to expand on their
views with regard to drugs education, drug-use experiences, and future
intentions for alcohol use/non-use. There was additionally a section in
which respondents could comment on any of the subjects covered in
the questionnaire. All open-ended questions were optional.

In-depth interviews

Although we received a lot of commentary on the questionnaires from
our sample and met all our respondents in their schools in the early
years, it was not until Year 4 that we were adequately resourced to
undertake in-depth interviews. We were able to interview eighty-six
volunteer subjects when they were 17 years old. These interviews went
extremely well and allowed young people, who normally only discuss
drug taking with friends, to provide us with often highly sophisticated

perspectives about their drug taking or abstention. Many implied that they felt able to be so open with us because of their on-going relationship with the research team and evidence that their views were taken seriously and held in complete confidence. Indeed many subjects chastised us for being so slow to undertake interviews. One male subject, when asked if our project had got to the central issues of drug use amongst young people, compared the interview and survey approaches and was in no doubt about the supremacy of the interview.

> I think it helps, it's a lot more . . . at the back of this one here [questionnaire] it asks if you've got any comments, please write them in. . . . I read this questionnaire and one of my mates had a look at it, and it's just not in depth enough. The interview can get it across more easily. [You don't think we're getting to the heart . . . ?] Not with the questionnaire, the interview's a lot better. You can just pick this up [questionnaire] and you don't know what the person's like, you don't know nothing about them, whereas if you meet somebody and get to know them a bit . . . it's much better. There's a question there somewhere, it's got four questions, either I do take drugs or I don't, and it doesn't give you the option to expand, it's like tick one box and that puts you in a category. This is a bit more flexible.
>
> (Tom, 17 years)

The interviews had several purposes. Firstly they allowed us to explore in far more detail the key issues thrown up by the survey findings of the first three years and in particular to seek more extensive and 'open' answers to 'why' and 'how' questions about drug use. Secondly the interviews allowed us to seek respondents' views on the efficacy of the questionnaires. We were able to ask whether respondents had filled them in accurately, whether they thought classmates had been honest and so on. We also asked interviewees some of the questions we had posed them in their fourth-year questionnaire and independently compared answers. Thirdly the interviews, by allowing respondents to place drinking and drug use in the wider context of their everyday lives, gave us far more insight into how they spent their leisure time, how they created 'time out' from work, domesticity, study or unemployment. Finally part of the interview explored future expectations. Did interviewees expect to begin or cease to take drugs or change their regularity of use? What were the factors which they felt would affect prospective drinking and drug use?

All the interviews were voluntary. They were undertaken by fully trained 'young' interviewers most of whom were brought up in the same regions as the respondents. The interviews were taped using a compact, battery-run tape recorder. They were later all transcribed. Most interviews took place in the respondent's home and the remainder in a quiet area of a leisure centre, library or public house. All interviews were one-to-one and conducted out of earshot of any third party. Respondents received a £10 music voucher for participating in these interviews which lasted between 45 and 90 minutes, and on average about an hour.

There were forty-six female and forty male interviewees of whom eighty-two were white. All of the original eight school populations were well represented and respondents came from the full range of socio-economic backgrounds.

In terms of their drugs status twenty-six of the sample had never tried an illicit drug and sixty had. There were twenty-five current users and seven were ex-users, having taken a drug but not expecting to do so again. The remainder were, at the time, reflecting on and reviewing their drugs status.

Most of the interview data will be presented in Chapters 4, 5 and 6, but in the next section we will illustrate what interviewees said about their experiences of filling in the annual questionnaire returns as we discuss validity and reliability.

Validity and reliability

In our view a well-conducted self-report survey, if it can demonstrate confidentiality and can present itself to young people (over the age of 13) as competent and 'streetwise', *is* the most cost-effective way of measuring alcohol and drugs prevalence and describing related behaviours. Ideally, however, these surveys should be set alongside interviews or focus groups which are more effective at teasing out subtleties, complexities and, more importantly, *contradictions*. A five-year longitudinal study throws up far more untidy data because it is obliged to measure people's ability to recall events over time and is also measuring, in this case, the impact of maturation in adolescence. Eighteen-year-olds often think 18 is an appropriate age to allow young people to drink in pubs but the same respondents in our research at the age of 16 nominated 16 as the right age. Thus if we compare the answers to this question for the same people over time we get quite different responses. We are not identifying a lack of validity in method here, or respondents lying, but a change of mind. So in this section we deliberately focus on anomalies and briefly discuss how we explain them, or not, in respect of validity and reliability.

Firstly we always applied the standard internal tests which have been discussed in detail elsewhere (Parker *et al.*, 1995). In Year 5, as in previous years, we employed two main methods for assessing possible under- and over-reporting of drug use. To assess under-reporting, we asked all respondents who did not report any drug taking whether, if they had tried an illegal drug, they would have admitted doing so in the questionnaire. In the complete Year 5 sample who had valid responses to this question, four respondents (1.8 per cent) indicated that they would not admit to drug use, and in the cohort with complete data for all five years eleven (2.1 per cent) indicated they would not admit to drug use. These figures are indicative of a high level of honest reporting.

To assess possible over-reporting, we included a (changing) 'dummy drug' item (e.g. 'nadropax' and 'penamine'), which only one respondent in the Year 4 sample (0.2 per cent) and two respondents in the Year 5 sample (0.4 per cent) claimed to have used. Thus, nearly all respondents distinguished between this dummy drug and all other listed drugs, a finding that is suggestive of honest reporting.

In Year 1 we had to disqualify as spoiled four returns where close scrutiny showed the respondents, one called David Bowie, were simply not taking the exercise seriously. There have been no spoiled returns since. However, having processed over 3,000 returns from nearly a thousand individuals we have inevitably identified anomalies. The most important ones refer to situations where an individual says in one year he or she took a drug but in a subsequent year or years contradicts this. One-off snapshot surveys do not have to deal with this process. We believe there were three main causes for anomalies in our study. Firstly, certainly in Year 1, there was some fabrication and over-reporting which later honest reporting contradicted. This was not only evident from analysing the survey data set but in the interviews respondents agreed that at 14 the first survey did capture some bravado.

> The first time we had this questionnaire, I thought it was a bit of a laugh. That's my memory of it, I can't remember if I answered it truthfully or not. I've got a feeling I did answer it truthfully, but I'm not sure. I've got a feeling I answered it seriously. It had a list of drugs and some of them I'd never heard of, and just the names just cracked me up.
>
> [Has your attitude changed as it's going on?] Yes. I think it's just the level of maturity. [Did you have any doubts about the confi-

dentiality of the answers you gave?] Yes. I still do. I'm not too bothered about it and I know that it wouldn't get back to my parents and that's the main thing, but the thing is, you can still get in touch with me now – you've still got my name and my phone number. [Interviewee reassured] I know that it wouldn't get back to my parents, that's not the problem at all, I'd just like to know how you're swinging it.

(Tom, 17 years)

The second reason for anomalous reporting is related to inaccurate reporting due to the level of commitment and concentration of the completer. If the questionnaire is too demanding, too boring, too long or if the respondent has not been given the appropriate introduction to and significance of a question, then young people may well treat it lightly. The most obvious sign of this is missing data. Levels of missing data declined dramatically from Year 1 to Year 5. In our research missing data was initially most problematic with our attempts to measure *exactly* how much people drank in a drinking session:

> [Looking back, were there any questions you might have answered dishonestly?] Only the ones about drink because I couldn't remember about the last time or how much, but I didn't do it on purpose, I just couldn't remember, so I just took it from the last time I remembered.
> [Did you underestimate?] I couldn't remember the quantity, so I just took it from the time I remember how much. [Underestimate it?] No probably not, because in school it [drinking pattern] was all the same, exactly the same every week.

(Anne, 18 years)

The third cause of anomalous reporting, which is specifically a feature of longitudinal 'cohort' research, is the redefinition or reconstruction of past events through time. For instance a single puff of cannabis reported at 14 is, a couple of years later, disregarded as an actual drug-taking episode, particularly by a subsequent 'expert' regular user. The strongest evidence that this reconstruction process is widespread comes from the interviewees whom we actually confronted with some examples and which they often explained and 'understood' in this way. When we look at the survey data we find that 27.2 per cent of the anomalous reporting we identified in relation to reported drug use between the first and fourth years of the survey were related to solvent (and gas) use – the archetypal ambiguous 'drug' used almost exclusively as an experimental substance in early adolescence. It is a classic experience to review and redefine in later years such use as 'kids' stuff'. Thus an early quick sniff of glue at the age of 14 may be reinterpreted as a non-event in light of later knowledge of others' more 'sophisticated' and purposive solvent use involving inhalation through bags or tubes. It was also notable that ex-users at the age of 17 (who had reported trying a drug at 14 or 15 but were now abstainers) produced a disproportionate number of anomalies. Again this is highly suggestive of a process also identified by Plant and colleagues (1985) and Fillmore (1988) of rescripting one's earlier (often embarrassing) adolescence to diminish cognitive dissonance as one settles for a particular personal identity upon entering young adulthood. Reforming biographies is a topic close to the heart of researchers using longitudinal-survey techniques (Collins *et al.*, 1985).

In conclusion, although we have identified some anomalous reporting, it may be less significant in terms of issues of reliability and validity and more significant as an opportunity for us to engage in creative understanding of the meaning that young people bring to both their drug use and to their opportunities to document that use in a questionnaire return. Some contradictions emanated from early misreporting, some from imprecision or confusion and some from personal 'reconstruction'. Even though we identified these three possible reasons for anomalous reporting through exploring the data, they simultaneously resonate with common-sense explanations of why young people might occasionally misreport on sensitive issues.

Summary

The North-West Longitudinal Study involved following several hundred young people from Year 1 when they were 14 years old for five years until they were 18. The overall aim of this study was to assess how 'ordinary' young people, growing up in England in the 1990s, developed attitudes and behaviours in relation to the unprecedented ready availability of drugs alongside other consumption options such as alcohol and tobacco. Their drugs status was to be situated in a broader analysis of their leisure 'time out' pursuits, and equally importantly within their maturation during adolescence.

This investigation involved the use of both quantitative and qualitative methods. The primary technique was a self-report questionnaire administered personally by the researchers to several hundred young people initially within eight State secondary schools (and then by post) in two, non-inner-city, boroughs of metropolitan north-west England.

In Year 1 the sample was representative of those areas by gender, socio-economic status and ethnicity. However attrition partly reduced this over time with the disproportionate loss of some 'working-class' participants and some respondents from Asian and Muslim backgrounds. However, there are strong indications that the 'core cohort' which has been with the project throughout the five years is very similar to the larger annual samples particularly in Years 4 and 5.

A longitudinal study is able to address issues of validity and reliability far more extensively than one-off snapshot surveys but in turn must also explain 'anomalous' or inconsistent reporting that occurs over the years. Although we believe that 'misreporting' was not a major problem there is good evidence that most anomalies were created as the participants became more honest and reliable each year feeling able to trust the research team whom they saw annually and without any negative consequences such as a breach of confidentiality.

During Year 4, eighty-six respondents were interviewed in depth. The transcribed interviews were a particularly rich source of data through which we were able to place the use and non-use of drugs in the broader backcloth of everyday young lives in which education, training, work, leisure, friendships, courtships, domestic relationships and enjoying 'time out' at weekends were all explored. The interviews also acted as a validation technique for the surveys and a stimulus for the pathways analysis. Alongside these, but during Year 5, a small number of case studies of 'critical incidents' related to drugs, were undertaken prompted by respondents reporting significant events to the researchers.

By Year 4 we identified four distinctive drugs pathways which proved to be robust conceptual tools. These pathway groups were regular *current drug users*, *abstainers* who had never used nor intended to use illicit drugs, *ex-triers* who had experimented with drugs but did not intend to do so again and a large group *in transition*. Those in transition may or may not have used an illicit drug but believed it possible or likely that they would do so in the future.

This pathway analysis provides a far more sophisticated conceptualisation of how young people develop attitudes and behaviours through time. In particular it distinguishes between drug experimenters, regular drug users and those who have never tried an illicit drug whilst showing how these behaviours are both dynamic yet remain linked to many other attitudes and attributes as will be seen in subsequent chapters.

3 Alcohol
'Our favourite drug'

We start our story about young people and drugs by focusing on their favourite drug, alcohol. This is because alcohol is usually the first and the most widely consumed psycho-active drug by young people in the UK and in fact its consumption is legal for young people over the age of 5. It is also one type of drug use which British youth share with their elders. Indeed, we can see that drinking is already normalised: it is the most widely practised form of recreational drug use in the UK (Royal College of Psychiatrists, 1986).

In this chapter we look at the stability in levels of adolescent drinking documented in the 1970s and 1980s before identifying important changes which have been occurring in the 1990s. We then turn our attention to our own respondents' drinking profiles and patterns and discuss the numerous ways in which the young people in this study mirror these national changes. When we look at the products young people drink, how often, how much and where, it appears that our sample is fairly typical of contemporary youth. Alongside these patterns of alcohol consumption we will attempt to illustrate the meaning and significance attached to drinking alcohol, going to pubs, socialising with friends, having 'good times' and 'bad times', and alcohol's role in young people's leisure-time experiences.

Whatever pathway status young people take, whether they drink or not, whether they take illicit drugs or not, they almost invariably talk about the importance of 'time out' from everyday life, of socialising with their friends, having a good time, having a laugh and relaxing from the stresses and worries they feel. For most young people alcohol is a key component of this 'time out' and it is this centrality to their leisure which makes alcohol the 'favourite drug' for our respondents. Within the range of approaches to drinking evident in this study there is a spectrum from abstainer to heavy drinker, from occasional celebratory drinking with families to regular poly drug use of a wide repertoire of legal and illicit drugs in pubs, clubs and parties. Whilst some young people express concern about their own or their friends' or relatives' drinking, most by and large see their bad experiences, hangovers and drink-related problems as a necessary downside to alcohol consumption.

Patterns, past and present

An overview of recent research regarding trends in young people's drinking across Britain over the last three decades will provide us with the backdrop upon which to situate the drinking patterns of our respondents as they move through adolescence.

By looking at how much young people drink, how often, which drinks are consumed, where, from what age and with whom we are able to build up a profile of adolescent drinking. In general the 1970s and 1980s have been characterised as decades of apparent stability in young people's drinking (May, 1992; Duffy, 1991), although periods of public concern occurred within them. There were moral panics around issues of under-age drinking both in and away from licensed premises, drink-related disorder, the emergence of 'lager louts' in the Home Counties and 'champagne charlies' in the City, public drinking, the role of alcohol in football 'hooliganism', and the scale of young people's drinking on continental holidays (Marsh and Fox Kibby, 1992; Tuck, 1989; Marsh *et al.*, 1978).

The 1990s, by comparison, have been characterised by signs of change in young people's alcohol consumption. Three areas of apparent change include frequency of drinking, quantities of alcohol consumed and types of alcoholic drinks favoured by young people, with the introduction of designer drinks, high-strength bottled lagers and ciders, fortified wines, 'alcopops' and mixer drinks aimed at the youth market (Brain and Parker, 1997; Measham, 1996).

Given the problematic nature of comparisons of the findings of alcohol research, there are clear limitations to an attempt at the identification of patterns of continuity and change in young people's drinking behaviour. The complexities, limitations and lack of comparability of research looking at alcohol consumption by adults are increased when looking at young people and particularly for what is such a widespread, regular, legal and socially acceptable activity. The two main methodological types of alcohol research, the quantitative and the qualitative, each have their own limitations. School-based quantitative surveys are affected by whether administrators are teachers or external researchers, smartly or casually dressed and so on.

Household-based quantitative surveys of young people face problems of privacy when conducted in the parental household and issues of sample representativeness and the exclusion of non-household-based teenagers such as those living in local authority care, in hostels or homeless. Qualitative studies of young people's drinking are rarer, less well funded, less generalisable by definition and currently no longer *en vogue*. Both qualitative and quantitative alcohol studies face problems of lack of comparability relating to under-reporting, over-reporting, faulty recall, reinterpretation of previous events and experiences over a period of time, and methodological issues regarding alcohol-consumption measures in general and the standardisation of units of measurement in particular, especially in self-reported drinking (Lemmens, 1994; Miller *et al.*, 1991; Turner, 1990). Nevertheless, given its legality and availability, information can be more easily gathered on alcohol than on illicit drugs. Thus a third source of information on drinking is 'official' statistics on the manufacture, sale and consumption of alcohol collated by drinks manufacturers, the marketing industry and associated trade organisations, some of which will be of relevance to young people's drinking.

The 1970s and 1980s

With little large-scale alcohol research conducted before the 1970s and even fewer studies which included young people, our first impressions of youthful drinking date from the 1970s and increase with more detailed surveys being administered during the 1980s. The first national survey focusing on young people's alcohol consumption was *Adolescent Drinking*, conducted in 1984 (Marsh *et al.*, 1986). Further quantitative studies by academic researchers, the Health Education Authority, the Department of Health and the OPCS added to the picture of youthful drinking in the late 1980s.

Despite the problems of comparability raised earlier, it is worth noting the consensus on some of the broad patterns in adolescent behaviour and attitudes surrounding alcohol found in the research of the 1970s and 1980s. From primary school age when young children developed negative and 'moralistic' attitudes to alcohol (Fossey, 1992; Jahoda and Cramond, 1972) they began to change their perceptions of drinking at around secondary school age and started linking alcohol with images of adulthood, sociability and excitement (Aitken, 1978). The average age young people had their first alcoholic drink was at about 10 for boys and 12 for girls. At around the age of 13 occasional drinking developed, most usually at home supervised by parents during family celebrations and holidays. By the age of 14–15 young people's drinking increased from occasional to more regularly, with about four or five in ten at this age having had an alcoholic drink within the week prior to the research. A considerable number of young people by this age had moved away from parentally supervised home-based drinking to obtaining alcohol from off-licence premises, either directly or indirectly, and consuming it with peers in streets, parks and private parties. At this point in the development of youthful drinking, the consumption of cheap ciders, beers and fortified wines for maximum levels of intoxication may have been favoured. By the age of 16–17 only a very small percentage of young people had not had an alcoholic drink and growing numbers were drinking in licensed premises with friends on an occasional or regular basis (e.g. Plant *et al.*, 1990; Marsh *et al.*, 1986; Plant *et al.*, 1985; Hawker, 1978). The frequency and quantity of alcohol consumed increased throughout the teens to a peak of nearly eight in ten women having had a drink in the past week at 18 and nearly nine in ten men having had a drink in the past week at 20, linked to marital status, children, disposable income and opportunities for drinking (Goddard, 1991; Goddard and Ikin, 1988).

Although national alcohol consumption figures remained fairly stable throughout the 1970s and 1980s there were substantial varia-tions in drinking patterns when looking at population groups differentiated by gender, race, religion, age, social class, marital status, geographic region and so on. The north and north-west of England, for example, had the highest levels of male and female weekly alcohol consumption (Plant and Plant, 1992)

The 1990s onwards

Against this historic backcloth of overall stability in the patterns of youthful alcohol consumption there have been several changes in young people, leisure and drinking styles during the 1990s. There are indications of changes in relation to sessional consumption, light/occa-sional drinking, the manufacture and marketing of alcoholic drinks, the development of licensed premises, the rise of illicit and poly drug use, and the dynamic impact of gender and race on young people's drinking behaviour and attitudes.

One of the key changes of the 1990s has been in the arena of young people's leisure-time pursuits and opportunities. The emergence of the 'rave' dance music scene in the late 1980s and its continuation in a strong dance club culture throughout the 1990s (Collin, 1997) has led to a club-based leisure industry with an increase in the availability and consumption of recreational 'dance drugs' such as ecstasy and amphetamines, combined with a rise in the purchase of soft drinks at the expense of alcohol sales (Measham *et al.*, 1998). The Henley Centre for Forecasting estimated that attendance at 'rave' events was over 50 million a year in Britain in 1993, with each person spending an average of £35 per evening on admission charges, soft drinks and 'dance drugs'. In the same year the value of the 'rave' market as a whole was calculated to be £1.8 billion (Thornton, 1995: 15).

Alongside the booming dance club culture other leisure facilities have attracted young customers including the growing number of public and private gyms, sports centres, multi-screen cinemas, restaurants and electronic games arcades. These new youth leisure facilities, combined with a switch from licensed to off-licence sales (with the increase in home drinking, home entertainments, the emergence of satellite and cable television and home video viewing) have all resulted in decreased spending in pubs by young people.

The identification of a reduction in on-licence sales of alcohol by the drinks manufacture and marketing industries, and less spending by young people in pubs in particular, led to attempts to revitalise the youth drinks market in three main ways. Firstly drinking venues were updated and refurbished for the youth market and set up in competition with the leisure-time alternatives for young people. This is evident in the introduction of a range of licensed premises including 'fun' pubs, themed pubs, wine bars, speciality beer pubs, continental-style café bars and pub entertainments such as satellite sports television, personality DJs, live music, comedy, karaoke, quiz nights and so on. The drinks companies became increasingly sophisticated in their targeting and marketing of pubs to specific sections of the population such as town teenagers, students, 'twentysomethings', older traditional drinkers, young families and so on, using the location of pubs, their decor, ambience and the range of food, drinks and entertainments on offer to carve out a niche for their chain.

Secondly the drinks industry introduced new alcoholic drinks whose distinct designs and marketing were aimed at the youth market. In the early 1990s strong bottled white ciders and premium lagers were directed at young drinkers along with fortified wines and aperitifs. These were followed after 1995 by the alcoholic lemonades and colas now known as 'alcopops', and 'ice' lagers and ciders whose strength was increased through the manufacturing process. The lucrative dance club market was tapped through the introduction of updated soft drinks: isotonic drinks, mineral waters, and high caffeine and 'energy' drinks for those young people who preferred not to drink alcohol at dance events. The drinks industry pushed further into the dance club market with the introduction of sophisticated club cocktails, aperitifs, wine and spirit mixers and alcoholic 'energy' drinks with added herbal extracts such as guarana, combined with the sponsorship of dance club events and alcohol promotion nights (Measham *et al.*, 1998). Such was public concern over their apparent popularity with young people that some licensed premises stopped selling the new 'alcopops' and the drinks industry reluctantly introduced a voluntary code regulating the packaging and advertising imagery used in the marketing of 'alcopops' (Brain and Parker, 1997).

Thirdly alongside the manufacture and marketing of new alcoholic and soft drinks for young people there has been an across-the-board increase in the average alcohol by volume strength of drinks sold in the 1990s. Studies of young people's drinking since the mid 1990s have confirmed the growing popularity of this new generation of stronger alcoholic beverages such as bottled white ciders, premium and 'ice' lagers, fortified wines and aperitifs aimed at the youth market (e.g. Hughes *et al.*, 1997; Health Education Authority, 1996; Measham, 1996; McKeganey *et al.*, 1996; the Scottish Council on Alcohol, 1996).

Young people's drinking and drug use are not mutually exclusive, however, with evidence of some young people combining alcohol with illicit recreational drugs during their leisure time. Such combined drug use is in part dependent on the social situation and desired effects of use. So for example, alcohol and cannabis may be favoured combination drugs in relaxed home settings whereas alcohol and amphetamines or 'poppers' are reportedly used together in a range of club settings.

Research has shown evidence of some emerging patterns in relation to youthful drinking which are only in part the result of changes in the marketing of pubs and alcohol. There appears to be a polarisation of drinking behaviour with numbers of occasional and light drinkers increasing alongside consumption levels by heavy drinkers. For example, an increase in light/occasional drinking and in the numbers of non-drinkers has been identified by Balding and Regis (1996) for both girls and boys in the 11–15-year-old age group.

Amongst more frequent drinkers, the proportion of young people who drink on at least a weekly basis does not appear to be rising during the 1990s. However, weekly drinkers do appear to be drinking more alcohol per week. Balding and Regis (1996) found an increase in the number of standard alcohol units per week consumed by weekly drinkers in 1990–94 and this was confirmed by Goddard (1996) and

Miller and Plant (1996). Whilst acknowledging the critical issue of accuracy of measurement, research suggests that changing drink preferences alongside changing attitudes to intoxication are leading to increased sessional consumption by weekly drinkers (Measham, 1996). Amongst these weekly drinkers are a minority of heavy, regular and problematic young drinkers who routinely drink up to and indeed beyond the current 'sensible' drinking guidelines and have been identified as more likely to engage in various sorts of risk taking or 'deviant' behaviour. The links between alcohol, smoking, under-age sexual intercourse, illicit drug use, violence, disorder and criminal behaviour have been discussed more fully elsewhere (Newcombe *et al.*, 1994; Plant and Plant, 1992). It should be noted here, however, that not all heavy end alcohol use and 'abuse' can be linked to socio-economic and psychological problems. There is increasing evidence that young 'risk takers' are predominantly 'normal' in their psychological assessment scores and are more curious, outgoing, sociable and pleasure-seeking than their risk-avoiding peers. Not only do these 'risk takers' question rules and authority, not surprisingly, they also have impressive educational attainments, and are increasingly likely to be females and from middle-class backgrounds too (Leitner *et al.*, 1993) than previously was supposed (Plant *et al.*, 1985).

Finally in this section we consider the changing nature of the impact of gender and race on drinking behaviour amongst young people in Britain. There is some evidence to suggest that young women in the 1990s are closing the teenage gender gap in drinking during the early and mid teens with few significant differences in frequency and quantity of consumption at this age. Young women have a greater disposable income and there is evidence that they are adopting working and behavioural patterns such as drinking and smoking which were traditionally seen as more male-oriented (Rowlands *et al.*, 1997). Choice of drink remains highly gendered, however, illustrating how drinking alcohol is linked with self-image, identity and consumer marketing for young people. Women and men also discuss their drinking in different terms, with themes such as self-control versus disinhibition suggesting that gendered attitudes to drinking continue. The gender gap in frequency and quantity of consumption re-emerges during early adulthood, however, with young women's drinking peaking at around 18 then declining thereafter. Men's drinking continues to increase and peaks later at around 20 then stabilises rather than declines during the mid twenties (Goddard and Ikin, 1988), although we should not be surprised if these patterns are redefining at the end of the millenium.

Race and religion both exert significant influences on youthful drinking behaviour in Britain in the 1990s. In representative surveys of young people which include racial minorities in their sample, ethnic, religious and cultural factors amongst certain specific groups appear to delay the onset of regular drinking and of pub-based socialising. Muslims, for example, are significantly more likely to be abstainers than young people of other religious groups or those who hold no religious beliefs. The differences between white and Afro-Caribbean young people's self-reported drinking, however, are less significant (James *et al.*, 1997; Newcombe *et al.*, 1994).

From our consideration of general trends in adolescent drinking in the 1990s, we now turn to the present research to see how the respondents in this study compare. Our sample of young people was asked various questions on alcohol consumption both in their five annual questionnaires and also in the in-depth interviews. The following section discusses some of the key findings in relation to onset of drinking, frequency, quantity, types of drink, location, reasons for drinking, positive and negative experiences after drinking, and typical and ideal leisure-time scenarios, obtained by using these quantitative and qualitative methods.

The North-West Study: alcohol through adolescence

Onset of drinking

In the first year of the study at the age of 14–15 nine in ten respondents reported having tried an alcoholic drink at least once in their lives. The average age of their first drink was 11, with a slight gender difference: boys tried their first drink at approximately 10.7 years old and girls tried their first drink at approximately 11.9 years old. As Table 3.1 illustrates, over the course of the five years of the study almost all respondents came to have tried an alcoholic drink: at the age of 14, 90.2 per cent of young people had tried alcohol and this rose to 96.8 per cent by the age of 18. A core 3.2 per cent of our sample continued to totally abstain from alcohol up to the age of 19.

Drinking frequency

Throughout the five years of the study, frequency of alcohol consumption was assessed by asking respondents to estimate how often they *usually* drink alcohol. Methodological issues relating to the usefulness of the usual drinking frequency question with youthful respondents

Table 3.1 Respondents ever having tried an alcoholic drink (%)

	Year 1 n = 776	Year 2 n = 752	Year 3ᵃ n = 523	Year 4 n = 536	Year 5 n = 529
No	9.8	7.4	5.0	4.7	3.2
Yes	90.2	92.6	95.0	95.3	96.8
Total (n)	776	752	521	536	529
(%)	(100)	(100)	(100)	(100)	(100)

Note:
ᵃ Missing: two answers in Year 3.

are discussed in detail elsewhere (Aldridge and Measham, forth-coming). Respondents' self-reported usual drinking frequency from the age of 14 to 19 is shown in Table 3.2. Answers were grouped together in five categories of response: weekly, monthly and occasional drinkers, those who had tried an alcoholic drink but no longer drank alcohol and those who had never tried alcohol. Our findings show how over the course of the teenage years covered by this study young people move from an occasional alcoholic drink to much more frequent drinking, with the majority of respondents developing into weekly drinkers by the time they reach the age of 18. Thus 29.9 per cent of the young people in our sample considered themselves to usually drink alcohol at least weekly at the age of 14 but this rose to 80.2 per cent by the age of 18. Monthly drinkers who reported that they usually drank alcohol less than once a week but once a month or more fell from nearly a quarter of the sample at the age of 14 to 10.8 per cent by the age of 18. Occasional drinkers (who drank less than once a month) fell from almost one-third of young people at the age of 14 to under 5 per cent by the age of 18. Non-drinkers (including both those who had tried alcohol at least once and those who had never tried it) fell from 13.8 per cent at the age of 14 to 4.4 per cent of the sample at 18.

Figure 3.1 shows the five years' trend towards more frequent drinking in graphic form. The rising peak frequency of consumption across the five years of the study is clear, with most young people drinking two or three times a week by the age of 18, usually on Friday and Saturday nights.

Each group identified by their reported usual drinking frequency

Table 3.2 Usual drinking frequency (%)[a]

	Year 1 n = 776	Year 2 n = 752	Year 3 n = 523	Year 4 n = 536	Year 5 n = 529
Weekly	29.9	40.7	56.6	72.1	80.2
Monthly	23.9	26.4	24.2	15.1	10.8
Occasional	32.4	22.8	12.1	6.2	4.6
Ex-drinker	3.9	2.7	2.1	1.9	1.1
Abstainer	9.9	7.5	5	4.7	3.2
Total (n)	769	747	521	535	526
(%)	(100)	(100)	(100)	(100)	(100)

Note:
[a] Missing: seven in Year 1, five in Year 2, two in Year 3, one in Year 4, three in Year 5.

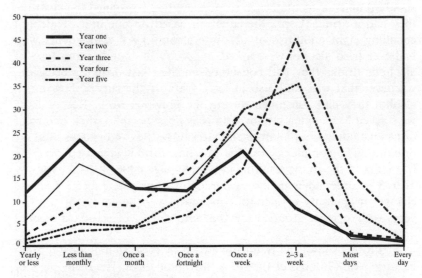

Figure 3.1 Changes in usual drinking frequency over five years (%)

had significantly different profiles, with the differences between abstainers and drinkers being the greatest. Weekly drinkers were more likely to try their first alcoholic drink at an earlier age and consumed greater quantities of alcohol on their last drinking occasion. They drank with their friends in public places, streets, nightclubs and at their own and friends' houses and were less likely to drink alcohol with their parents. Weekly drinkers reported both more positive and more negative experiences after drinking than their less frequently drinking peers. More frequent drinking was also linked to various indicators of 'deviance' including lifetime prevalence of illicit drug use, drink-related sexual experiences and contact with the police. Abstainers were more likely to be Asian and Muslim.

Quantity of alcohol consumed

Alongside frequency of drinking, a second key measure of alcohol consumption is the amount consumed. Given the methodological difficulties in structuring such a question, the format was refined throughout the course of the study to reflect the widening choice of alcoholic drinks available to young people in the early to mid 1990s, allowing us to calculate as accurately as possible the total number of standard units of alcohol each respondent had consumed the last time they had a drink. (Using the equation based on one unit of alcohol equalling eight millilitres of absolute alcohol.) All respondents who had ever tried alcohol were asked to specify the number and type of alcoholic drinks they had consumed on their last drinking occasion, whenever that was, and also in later years of the survey, how much alcohol they had consumed during the previous week. Respondents were asked to include as many details as possible about their choice of drinks including brand names and sizes of bottles and glasses used for drinking. The complexity of this question format increased over the five years of the study, resulting in a three-page table of drink types by Year 5 in order to maximise accuracy of response. Table 3.3 shows changes in quantity of alcohol consumed over the course of the five years with answers grouped together into ranges of standard alcohol units.

Figure 3.2 shows the trend towards heavier sessional consumption between Years 1 and 5 of the study in graphic form. The rising peak of medium and heavy consumption of over five units of alcohol on last drinking occasion clearly contrasts with the decline in light sessional drinking of under five units.

There was little change in the overall mean level of alcohol

Table 3.3 Quantity of alcohol consumed on last drinking occasion (%)

Units of alcohol	Year 1	Year 2	Year 3	Year 4	Year 5
1 – 2	29.2	21.9	17.5	14.1	13.9
3 – 4	18.4	15.4	16.6	20.1	12.7
5 – 6	9.2	9.5	12.3	11.9	14.9
7 – 10	16.8	20.5	21.6	20.3	22.3
11 – 20	13.1	23.4	24.4	27.2	23.9
21 – 28	6.0	5.1	4.5	4.2	8.4
29 – 40	3.0	2.7	2.9	1.2	2.8
41 +	4.4	1.5	0.2	1.0	1.0
Overall mean units	10.1	9.5	9.1	9.3	10.6
Overall modal units	2	2	1	4	2

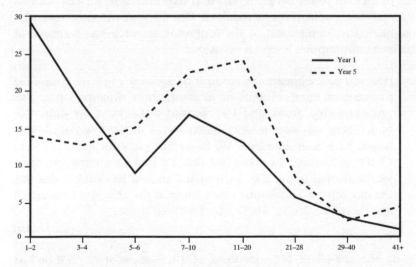

Figure 3.2 Changes in quantity of alcohol consumed on last occasion over five years (%)

consumption on last occasion reported by young people throughout their teens. Throughout the five years of the study respondents reported drinking an average of about nine or ten units the last time they had a drink. At each stage the modal (most frequent) response was between one and four units of alcohol. The low mean and mode in Year 3 may reflect the loss of heavy end drinkers in the sample due to attrition (see Chapter 2). Increases in Years 4 and 5 reflect more conservative young people remaining in the sample after Year 3 who increased their drinking after the age of 16, coupled with a move to drinking in licensed premises. If we look in more detail at the table and group the results into light, medium and heavy sessional consumption, the proportion of the sample at each year who were light sessional drinkers decreased whilst medium and heavy sessional drinking increased over the five years. Light sessional drinking of one to four units decreased from 48 per cent at the age of 14 to 27 per cent by the age of 18. Medium sessional drinking of five to ten units increased from 26 per cent at 14 to 37 per cent at 18 and heavy sessional drinking of eleven to forty units increased from 22 per cent to 35 per cent respectively. Responses of over forty units of alcohol consumed during last drinking occasion are suspicious and may represent over-reporting; these were negligible after the first year.

Indeed if researchers and readers are sceptical of the large quantities of alcohol young people report that they consume, the respondents themselves are sometimes incredulous. One 18-year-old interviewed for the qualitative component of the longitudinal study was surprised at his own consumption levels on occasion.

> [Do you ever estimate the amount of alcohol you have consumed in terms of standard units of alcohol?] In a situation where I've got unfeasibly drunk and I've worked out how many units I've had. There was one instance when I was in the lower sixth so I would have been seventeen. We hired this place for our sixth form Christmas do and I worked out that I'd had something like three weeks alcohol in one day. I thought I should be drunk – this was the day after, at lunch time when I was at the chippy – I thought I should still be drunk. That's why I worked it out.
>
> (John)

By the age of 18 over one-third of the sample were classified as heavy sessional drinkers; that is, they had consumed eleven units of alcohol or more on their last drinking occasion. The profile of this group of heavy drinkers suggests that they were significantly more likely than light sessional drinkers to be male, to drink alcohol once a week or more frequently, to have tried illicit drugs and to be pupils at the schools located in working-class catchment areas. At the age of 18, 80 per cent of male drinkers and 80 per cent of female drinkers reported drinking more than the current 'sensible' sessional drinking guidelines of four and three units of alcohol respectively on their last drinking occasion.

Turning now to past week consumption for 18-year-olds, the average number of standard units of alcohol consumed by this age group in the previous week was twenty-five, with a mode of five units. Of those who drank alcohol in the week prior to completion of their Year 5 questionnaires, one in ten drank no more than four units, four in ten drank five to twenty units, three in ten drank twenty-one to forty units and a staggering 18 per cent reported drinking over forty units of alcohol during the previous week. Of male drinkers at the age of 18, 50 per cent reported drinking more than the current 'sensible' weekly drinking guidelines of twenty-eight units of alcohol during the previous week. Of female drinkers at the age of 18, 36 per cent reported drinking more than the current 'sensible' weekly drinking guidelines of twenty-one units of alcohol during the previous week.

Do young people themselves consider their drinking in terms of measuring the quantity of alcohol consumed in general, and counting standard units of alcohol in particular? Eighty-six respondents were interviewed on a one-to-one basis at around the age of 17. Whilst over nine in ten young people interviewed had heard of the term standard units of alcohol only seventeen respondents (22.5 per cent) ever applied this to themselves and attempted to estimate the amount they drank in terms of standard units. Of these, only four respondents ever set limits on their own drinking in terms of the number of standard units of alcohol they would consume. Two of these did so for driving purposes. One heavy-drinking young man who was interviewed was asked if he had heard of standard units of alcohol:

> Yes. What is it . . . one unit or something per pint or something? Measuring like driving and stuff. I haven't passed my test so it doesn't matter. I can just walk home or stagger, or someone else will carry me home. I know how many I've had because I'm on the floor.
>
> (Michael)

Given the longitudinal nature of this study we are able to consider whether those individuals who reported more frequent and heavier drinking in earlier years are the same individuals as those who report more frequent and heavier drinking in Year 5. Several earlier studies of adolescent drinking have shown low correlations between younger heavy drinkers and later heavy drinkers (Plant *et al.*, 1985). Looking firstly at the relationship between frequent drinking (twice a week or more often) in the early and later teens, over three-quarters (76.5 per cent) of more frequent drinkers at the age of 15 were also frequent drinkers at the age of 18. Turning then to heavy consumption (eleven units of alcohol or more on last drinking occasion) the relationship is less clear with under half (41.4 per cent) of heavy sessional drinkers at the age of 15 being also heavy sessional drinkers at the age of 18.

Types of drinks

The North-West Study found that the choice of drinks consumed by young people in this study reflects national findings regarding the prevalence of beer, lager and cider consumption, and in particular the popularity of strong bottled lagers and ciders.

Respondents were asked which alcoholic drinks they usually drank, which ones they consumed on their last drinking occasion and which were their three favourite drinks. Throughout the study between one-quarter and one-third of young people reported usually drinking cider, with slightly lower numbers reporting usually drinking lager. When respondents were asked which were their favourite alcoholic drinks, the majority of current drinkers were brand-name specific when considering their favourite drink. At the age of 15 for example, 18 per cent of respondents gave brand names of cider as their favourite drink and a further 8 per cent mentioned cider in general without specifying any brand names. Specific brands of lager were reported as their favourite drinks by 15 per cent and a further 8 per cent mentioned lager in general. After cider and lager, brand-named aperitifs and liqueurs were the third most popular group of drinks for 13 per cent of current drinkers although none mentioned them in general. The fourth most popular group of drinks was spirits, with 10 per cent mentioning specific brand names and a further 8 per cent mentioning spirits in general. Of all alcoholic drinks, both brand name and generic, the most popular drink was a brand of bottled strong white cider, with a strength of over 8 per cent alcohol by volume (Measham, 1996).

Table 3.4 shows the percentages of young people drinking each type of drink in their late teens, along with the average amount of alcohol consumed on the last occasion for each of these types of drink. Looking at drink choice on last drinking occasion at the age of 18, we can see that beers, lagers and ciders are significantly more popular than other alcoholic drinks with this age group. Over eight in ten young people report drinking beer, lager or cider the last time they had a drink and over a third had spirits. Over a quarter had at least one aperitif or glass of wine the last time they had a drink. 'Alcopops' are reportedly the *least* most likely alcoholic drink for 18-year-olds with only one in five having consumed alcoholic lemonade or cola on their last drinking occasion. Research by Brain and Parker (1997) confirms the popularity of ciders and lagers over and above 'alcopops', even two years later when a wider variety of 'alcopops' were manufactured and marketed. The picture which emerges refutes the recent demonisation of 'alcopops' by some sections of the media and public. Not only are 'alcopops' the least popular drink with this age group, they are also linked with the lowest levels of consumption by those who do choose to drink them. Lagers and ciders are the preferred drink for heavy sessional drinkers, with an average of nearly nine units of lager or cider consumed on the last occasion for the eight in ten drinkers who had those drinks. An average of five units of wine and spirits were consumed on last drinking occasion by those who drank wine and spirits. Under four units of aperitifs and 'alcopops' were consumed on last occasion by the two or three in ten young people who drank them.

Table 3.4 Type of alcoholic drink consumed on last drinking occasion and mean number of standard units of alcohol imbibed for each type of drink, for all current drinkers at age 18

	% n = 502	Mean standard alcohol units
Ciders/lagers/beers	81.7	8.6
Spirits	37.8	4.7
Aperitifs	29.7	3.7
Wine	27.5	5.2
'Alcopops'	19.9	3.7
Total [a]	100	10.6

Note:
[a] Percentages add up to more than 100 because some respondents drank more than one type of alcoholic drink on last drinking occasion.

Drinking locations

Regarding the location of youthful drinking episodes, previous alcohol research has identified a shift during the mid to late teens from home-based drinking supervised by parents to pub-based drinking with friends. This study included several questions relating to where our respondents drank alcohol and with whom. In the first three years of the study respondents were asked a general question regarding where they usually drink alcohol. In the latter two years of the study the question format was changed from a general to a specific question which asked respondents where they were the last time they drank alcohol. Whilst the general and specific questions are not directly comparable, Table 3.5 illustrates some of the changes in answers to these two questions over the five years of the study by looking at a selection of five key locations featured within the more extensive list of items in the questionnaire.

At the ages of 14 and 15 young people reported that their own home, followed by friends' houses, were the main places where they drank alcohol. The third most usual drinking location for young people at 14 and 15 was outside in the streets, parks and other public places. By the age of 16 there was a considerable increase in the numbers of young people drinking in licensed premises such as public houses and nightclubs alongside continued drinking at home and in friends' houses. The increase in public-house drinking occurs at around the same age as the decrease in public street drinking, most probably related to some young people's ability to gain entry to licensed

Table 3.5 Changes in selected places where alcohol is consumed (%)[a]

	Year 1	Year 2	Year 3	Year 4	Year 5
Home	77.5	83.7	87.2	20.4	18.2
Friends' houses	66.8	79.9	82.4	12.4	9.7
Outside/streets/parks	65.0	70.6	45.6	0.8	0.6
Clubs/discos	51.9	47.0	74.2	24.2	17.6
Pubs	46.3	69.1	86.7	49.5	59.9

Note:
[a] Question format changed from general drinking locations to specific last occasion drinking location in Year 4, hence percentages in earlier years add to more than 100. Five key locations from a list of fifteen are featured in this table

premises from the age of 16 and to obtain alcohol either directly from bar staff or via older-looking friends. This suggests that by the age of 16 young people prefer drinking in pubs to outside on the streets, but that they will drink on the streets when unable to gain access to pubs and unwilling or unable to drink at home.

By the age of 17 most young people are able to obtain alcohol in pubs and clubs, whether directly or indirectly. Nearly three-quarters of 17-year-old drinkers consumed their last alcoholic drink on licensed premises: half of young people had their last drink in a pub or bar and a quarter of them last drank alcohol in a nightclub. Another third of 17-year-olds had their last drink in either their own home or a friend's house, leaving less than 1 per cent of drinkers having had their last drink outside on the streets. This trend continues up to 18 so that by the time young people can legally purchase alcohol in licensed premises six in ten had their last drink in a pub, whereas under three in ten had their last drink in their own or their friends' homes. Negligible numbers drank outside.

Reasons for drinking

Drinking location illustrates how young people's drinking develops in the mid teens as a part of both their celebrations with family and their leisure-time socialising with friends. Although aware of the limitations and subjectivity of attempts at ascertaining reasons for drinking through the use of self-report questionnaires, we attempted to identify some of the reasons young people themselves give for why they drink alcohol. During the first three years of the study respondents were given a check list of various reasons for drinking alcohol compiled from answers given during piloting of the questionnaire with young people of a similar age. Table 3.6 summarises the main reasons given by 14–16-year-olds for drinking.

The importance of light/occasional, home-based, parentally supervised drinking is reflected at the ages of 14 and 15. The main reason for drinking given by two-thirds of drinkers was to celebrate special occasions including birthdays, weddings and seasonal festivals. The positive and sociable aspects of drinking were also given as reasons by between a quarter and half of young drinkers in their early teens: they say they drink because they find it fun, their friends drink alcohol, it makes them less shy and it helps them 'chat up' potential partners. We suggest that they enjoy the sociability of *who* they drink with rather than *where* they drink at this age, with understandably only 16.9 per cent of 14-year-olds seeing their enjoyment of the

Table 3.6 Reasons for drinking alcohol (%)

	Year 1	Year 2	Year 3
Special occasions	67.6	65.6	59.7
It's fun	44.1	49.5	44.6
Makes me less shy	40.1	44.6	38.5
Friends drink	33.1	28.9	21.9
Like being drunk	26.4	32.9	28.4
Boredom	20.0	22.3	14.4
Helps 'chat up' people	19.0	22.1	19.1
Like pubs and clubs	16.9	34.0	66.7
Alcohol is kept at home	7.1	5.8	5.5

atmosphere in pubs and clubs as a reason for drinking. Of some concern, however, is the consideration that over a quarter of 14-year-olds reported that they like being drunk and a fifth of them are drinking to relieve boredom.

By the age of 16, whilst the celebration of special occasions is still given as a key reason for drinking, the importance of the role of pubs and clubs in young people's social lives has surpassed this as a reason for drinking. The percentage of young people who report drinking alcohol because they like pubs and clubs increased from 16.9 per cent of drinkers at the age of 14 to 66.7 per cent by the age of 16. This mirrors pubs changing from one of the least usual to most usual specified drinking locations over the course of the teens in Table 3.5.

By way of comparison, the qualitative interviews with 17-year-old respondents also asked about reasons for drinking alcohol. The seven main reasons given to this open-ended question were: to socialise (58.3 per cent), for enjoyment (28.6 per cent), liking the taste (26.2 per cent), to relax (25 per cent), to get merry/drunk (22.6 per cent), to have a good time (16.7 per cent) and to increase confidence/reduce inhibitions (13.1 per cent). One 17-year-old young woman summed it up: 'It's a social thing, a friend thing. It makes you relax. I suppose it helps you have a good time as well, or a better time if you're having a crap time' (Sarah).

Alcohol, pubs, clubs and 'time out'

Despite declining brewery profits and sales in the on-licence trade and the closure of hundreds of pubs across Britain every year, licensed premises remain a central leisure-time location for young people in the mid 1990s, and as we have seen, the attraction of pubs and clubs is reportedly a key reason for drinking in the late teens. Turning our attention to the ways in which pubs, clubs and 'time out' are discussed alongside reasons for drinking in the qualitative data, one 17-year-old respondent summed up why he drank as 'basically I like it. I just like drinking. I like being drunk as well, but I just like sitting in a pub and drinking.' A heavy-drinking male respondent who drinks nearly every day said he drinks alcohol: 'When I'm socialising, I go out for a pint with my mates. It gets me out of the house. And I have a laugh while I'm having a drink, go for a game of darts or something' (Steven). One young woman interviewed who drinks pints of cider at her local pub links the taste, the effects and the pub itself as reasons for her drinking:

> I like getting drunk. I like the taste. Well, I used to like the taste of cider. I'm getting a bit sick of it now.
> [Why do you like getting drunk?] It makes me more outgoing.
> [Could you imagine going to the pub and not drinking alcohol?] Yes. Sometimes I just go and get a coke if I don't feel like drinking. But more often than not I do start drinking because you just go, order your pint and you sit down. . . . It's quite strange because before I was eighteen it was the only pub that didn't ask for ID because they don't expect young people to go in there because it's not a fashionable pub. . . . I get really loud when I'm drunk and it's not very nice really but they're all right about it.
>
> (Marie)

Public houses have been a central leisure location in Britain for 150 years, at least for working-class men, and alcohol has traditionally been the main focus of spare-time socialising within them (Harrison, 1971). Since the mid nineteenth century 'within the sphere of commercialized leisure . . . the pub played a central role' in Greater Manchester (Davies, 1992: 169). In the late twentieth century, despite changes in young people's lives and in the leisure industry, by and large the consumption of alcohol in pubs remains an integral part of British leisure as illustrated by this study, with adolescents developing into weekend pub drinkers during their mid teens, drinking alcohol in some form in pubs of some sort or other. With the extension of adolescence, the expansion of higher education, delayed entry into the labour market and later moving out of the parental home, the desire for a social space away from parents and siblings is heightened. Respondents in this study mentioned the possibility of open-air venues for socialising in summer (the beach was a regular spot for some of our sample in their mid teens), but pubs were one of the few alternatives to their own home on cold, dark and wet winter nights. Thus the continuing importance of pubs and bars in young people's lives reflects not only their historic attractions but also the lack of attractive, affordable local alternatives.

When discussing their reasons for drinking, some respondents interviewed illustrated the movement between the legal and illicit drugs markets in their selection of leisure time drug(s). In a world of increasing availability of illicit drugs, as we shall see in later chapters, decisions surrounding their drinking become entwined with decisions surrounding their use of other psycho-active drugs. Described elsewhere as a pick 'n' mix approach to recreational drug use (Parker and Measham, 1994), alcohol is only one of a range of possible drugs in young people's repertoires, although favoured by many because it is relatively cheap, legal, tolerated (and even facilitated) by many of their peers and elders, and is associated with youthful socialising and celebrating centring on pubs and clubs. For example, one young man said that his main reason for drinking was because 'it's a change . . . have a drink instead of having a smoke [of cannabis]', although he qualified this by saying that he prefers to smoke cannabis than drink alcohol if he has to drive, adding that 'I just don't really want to go out and get drunk on it [alcohol] all the time' (Martin).

Although not essential to it for all young people and certainly recognised as problematic to a greater or lesser extent by many, alcohol is part of the overall (p)leisure package embraced in modern youth culture. These 'good times' with alcohol do not come cheap, however. Amongst our interviewees who reported having a drink in the previous week, young women spent an average of £12 in the past week on alcohol and young men spent an average of £21.

Alcohol is a thread throughout young people's leisure times, the good and the bad. Hence it is no surprise that alcohol was the most popular drug amongst the young people interviewed. Of these eighty-six young people, those who had tried illicit drugs (69.8 per cent, n = 60) were asked whether they had a 'favourite drug' and if so, which one(s). One-third of interviewees who had tried drugs (33.3 per cent, n = 20) said that their favourite drug was (still) alcohol. Cannabis was their second favourite drug chosen by one-sixth of interview respondents (16.7 per cent, n = 10) and tobacco and ecstasy were joint third choice as favourite drugs (8.3 per cent each, n = 5). One person said amphetamines were her favourite drug. No other drugs were mentioned. It is interesting to note the proportion of young people who considered legal as well as illicit drugs in their replies when asked to name their 'favourite drug', with 41.7 per cent (n = 25) nominating alcohol or tobacco. Our respondents explain the reasons for their preference for alcohol below. For example, when asked which was his favourite drug one regular drug user said:

> Alcohol. Saying that, I'm not addicted to alcohol like I'm addicted to cigarettes. I really enjoy going out and getting legless. Because it's so social. You can go out and you can have a really good time. That's very ambiguous but say I saw someone I didn't like and I was drunk, I'd go up to them and say 'All right? How are you doing?' It's very cheap for a start.
>
> [Availability?] Availability's brilliant. That's another thing. There's places set aside for you to drink – pubs – rather than like a smoking room so that's a bonus. I can do it with my family, because I'm very close to my family.
>
> [Where do you prefer to have it?] Pub. Especially when you've got a local.
>
> (John)

Alongside access, availability and legality, young people also expressed a preference for alcohol because of its predictability regarding its quality, strength and effects. One young woman explained how 'I know there's not going to be anything wrong with it and I know what sort of state I'll be in if I drink too much' (Tracy).

Furthermore, alcohol fits into a larger drug repertoire. Two-thirds of drug users in the interview sample had used more than one drug at the same time (n = 40) and almost all of these mentioned using a combination of drugs which included alcohol. Three-quarters of interviewees who reported having a 'favourite combination of drugs' described a combination repertoire which included alcohol. Thus, not all young people drink alcohol exclusively nor do they substitute illicit drugs for alcohol in their late teens; for some they develop poly drug repertoires in which alcohol is consumed alongside, before or after other drugs. During one-to-one interviews fifty-two different combinations of drugs were mentioned which included alcohol and at least one other drug: including cannabis (n = 18), tobacco (n = 11), amphetamines (n = 6), ecstasy (n = 4), LSD (n = 1) and poppers (n = 1). Forty-one of the fifty-two specified combinations involving alcohol combined with illicit drug use. Such alcohol/poly drug use may be actively sought for specific effects by some respondents. However, there were also some young people included in this group of alcohol and illicit drug users for whom alcohol acted as a disinhibitor leading to unplanned and potentially more dangerous poly drug use. This is illustrated in the comments of one female drug user who said the main thing which helped her make up her own mind about taking drugs was that 'I was drunk at the time as well and I think that made a hell of a difference, because when you're sober you've just got a different perspective on it totally' (Zoe).

This acknowledgement from young people that they themselves see alcohol and tobacco as drugs may in part be an indication of the success of health education in schools on this subject and also in part result from their perspectives on their parents and elders' preference for legal rather than illicit drugs. Their discussion of legal and illicit drugs in relation to their perspectives on 'time out' suggests an interchangeability for many, depending on their circumstances, situation and mood. The importance of 'time out' is evident in many of the answers given by young people who were interviewed and asked about their spare time, their ideal weekend and their ideal leisure location. Most young people's ideal weekend included several features from a general programme whose similarity is evident in the following five quotes from a variety of young women and men interviewed: 'going out clubbing Friday night. Spending Saturday morning in bed. Go into town clothes shopping Saturday afternoon. Probably going to the pictures Saturday night. And then sleeping Sunday and then going out somewhere for the afternoon' (Sandra). Or 'going out to clubs. All nighters. A lot to drink. Drink on one night, drugs on the other night and then a mellow Sunday, just chill out Sunday' (Andy). Or 'go to the pub on the Friday night. Go to a football match on the Saturday and Saturday night go to a club. [Sunday?] Sleep' (Laura). Or 'just going out to a club, getting drunk, having a laugh. I just like going out. I like going out with the girls. I like going out, getting drunk and everything, acting the fool' (Jenny). Or:

> Friday – I reckon go to the pub on the Friday, bit of a piss up and then probably go back to someone's house, sit around. Then sleep all day Saturday and do nothing and just eat, and then go out to town and have a good night out, and then not work on Sunday which is what I normally do. Just relax really.
>
> (Liam)

A similar formula was in evidence when we asked young people about their ideal leisure location. Whilst there were some interesting and unusual answers which would challenge any leisure company (such as synthesized, Ibiza-style, tropical holiday resorts), the most usual response was an appeal for some sort of integral entertainments site available under one roof and open up to twenty-four hours a day, which we have called the 'pleasure dome'. Within this 'pleasure dome' young people requested a wide range of entertainments, services, sports and leisure facilities including multi-screen cinemas, a variety of café bars and pubs, fast food chains, upmarket restaurants, pizza parlours, one or more night clubs, bowling alley, electronic games arcade, quaser, shops, sports centre, swimming pool and so forth. Young people favoured the town/city centre rather than out of town for their multi-complex dream leisure location, well served by public transport facilities and trustworthy security staff. Whilst tolerating the possibility of families and young children in their 'pleasure dome' in the day time, many were explicit in their preference for a venue specifically oriented towards young adults in the evening. A few went further in their fantasies and included the sale of certain 'soft' drugs which they considered acceptable in specific venues, reminiscent of Amsterdam-style cannabis cafés. 'Not allowing people over forty in' would bring a new twist to proof-of-age cards currently promoted by adult worlds.

Having considered the social context for young people's drinking we now discuss their own assessment of alcohol, its positive and negative effects.

Positive effects of drinking

Some quantitative details were obtained regarding young drinkers' views about the effects of drinking alcohol, both positive and negative. Alongside reasons for drinking, detailed questions on how young people felt after they had been drinking were included in the first three years of the questionnaire, although it is recognised that reasons for drinking and effects of drinking clearly overlap. (These questions were omitted in the last two years of the study for reasons of space, due to the changing focus of the questions.) Tables 3.7 and 3.8 contain details of the self-reported positive and negative effects of alcohol for 14–16-year-olds. It is clear that even at the age of 14 the majority of young drinkers enjoy having a drink: over eight in ten feel happy and have a good time after drinking. Over three-quarters of them feel more at ease with their friends after drinking and, perhaps of more concern,

Table 3.7 Self-reported positive experiences after drinking (%)

	Year 1	Year 2	Year 3
Felt happy	87.6	92.2	95.7
Had a good time	82.1	90.1	93.8
At ease with friends	77.8	84.3	88.2
At ease with strangers	53.9	65.4	78.7

over half of them also feel more at ease with strangers. Whilst feeling more at ease with strangers is included here with positive effects of alcohol consumption, the negative impact of an effect such as this is clear. Respondents may consider such a quality as positive in that it facilitates meeting and mixing with their peers but it also raises issues of personal safety and vulnerability for young people under the influence of alcohol at the age of 14, particularly in public drinking locations where they are not supervised by older relatives or friends.

By the age of 16 almost all young people report enjoying alcohol at least sometimes when they drink. Around nine in ten drinkers feel happy, more at ease with friends and have a good time after drinking alcohol. Nearly eight in ten report also feeling more at ease with strangers. This is hardly surprising, given the way alcohol acts primarily as a depressant drug, slowing the rate of activity of the central nervous system, hence resulting in feelings of relaxation, disinhibition, confidence and enjoyment in social situations for drinkers.

Negative effects of drinking

In general fewer young people report negative than positive experiences after drinking alcohol. Table 3.8 shows the percentages of 14–16-year-olds for the ten highest reported negative experiences from a list of items included in the questionnaire, a list which included effects which could be considered negative in some way either physically or emotionally. Over a third of drinkers had experienced eight of the listed negative experiences at least sometimes when they had a drink. The most frequently reported negative repercussion of drinking was that young people were unable to remember some aspect of their drinking occasion the next day. From the age of 14 approximately six in ten drinkers sometimes forgot things after drinking. Around four or

five young drinkers reported negative physical effects which might indicate a considerable quantity of alcohol was consumed: they had a
headache, vomited, had a 'hangover' and had fallen over after
drinking. About half of young people in their early to mid teens felt
guilty after drinking and about a third were worried about some sort
of sexual experience or encounter they had had after drinking. One-
quarter of young people had argued either with friends or relatives
after drinking and about one-fifth had had their own drinking criticised by others for some reason. Four in ten 14-year-olds and five in
ten 16-year-olds reported feeling unhappy at least sometimes after
drinking.

The qualitative interviews with respondents when they were aged 17
to 18 provided an opportunity for them to elaborate on the sorts of
experiences they had had after drinking, providing the details and the
context for their experiences, along with their own perspective and
understanding of these events. One young woman reflected on the
sorts of arguments she had with her boyfriend and her parents about
her drinking, the former also illustrating the gendered nature of
constraints on young people's drink-related behaviour:

Table 3.8 Self-reported negative experiences after drinking (%)[a]

	Year 1	Year 2	Year 3
Unable to remember things	58.3	58.3	58.9
Had headache	54.6	55.2	55.4
Been sick	40.6	43.6	52.4
Felt guilty	48.0	46.6	51.8
Had hangover	40.2	42.8	47.5
Felt unhappy	38.4	41.4	47.3
Fell over	52.6	50.7	45.0
Worried about sexual encounter	32.4	34.9	32.9
Had argument	28.0	24.7	25.6
Had drinking criticised	19.2	18.3	21.1

Note:
[a] The ten most common experiences (in Year 3) from a list of twenty-four negative
effects of alcohol are featured in this table.

We were absolutely ratted, stinking drunk, me and my friend and we were with my boyfriend and a couple of his friends. And we started being sick. We made a total show of ourselves and my boyfriend screamed at me the next day and told me to control myself. . . . It caused an argument. Once there was a time when my mum and dad caught me drinking. I told them I was staying for the weekend at a friend's but instead we camped out in the park. She found me in the park, drunk. I got grounded. . . . Sometimes if an argument has started I can sometimes get out of hand, I can take it a bit too far, when really you should just let it go. I tend to do more of that when I've had a drink.

(Vicky)

Another young woman who is a heavy sessional drinker hinted at the link between drinking and 'casual' sexual relationships, with alcohol acting as a disinhibitor for her:

I've gone completely all the way because I do know what I'm doing but you're drunk and you want to when you're drunk.
[Do you regret it afterwards?] Sometimes yes. 'What have I done, who's he?' . . . It's just like at a club on holiday last year I was going out with my boyfriend and I got up to no good. I told him three months later. You can't help it when you're on holiday.

(Jenny)

For young drinkers in general and young women in particular control emerged as an important theme. Issues of self-control, personal safety, vulnerability and risk were linked with both their own and others' intoxication. Whilst some young people wanted to lose control through their drinking and drug use, describing it in terms of 'losing it' or 'getting out of it' others clearly liked to feel intoxicated without crossing the threshold to total loss of control. For example, one poly drug user whose favourite drug is alcohol described how she had regulated her drinking on her last drinking occasion: 'Not overly [drunk]. We were drunk but more giggly. We weren't to the point where we didn't know what we were doing' (Sandra). Another respondent discussed drink-related casual sexual relationships, socialising with strangers and perceptions of risk during her interview:

You know when you're out and that and you're bladdered. And you think 'oh that person's gorgeous' and then you come home and you don't remember a thing. And then when you're out the next week people say 'that's the fella you got off with'. And you're just like 'oh I never'. That's happened a few times. I went back to some house once. I completely sobered up. I was on my own. I completely sobered up and I just shot off. I was out another time and I met these lads from Newcastle. And you know when you feel that someone's all right. And I went back to their hotel but they let me have one of their rooms on my own. They were dead sound. But a lot of my mates thought I was AWOL. Like when I came in they said 'oh they could have done anything to you, raped you or murdered you' and that. They never. I was lucky.

(Karen)

During the qualitative interviews three 17-year-olds, all female, revealed that they had consulted their doctors for problems which were in some way either directly or indirectly related to their drinking. One was generally 'run down', one had kidney problems which she thought were related to her use of ecstasy as well as alcohol, and the third young woman reported some sort of blood poisoning related to her alcohol consumption. 'I used to get bruises everywhere and it was from the drink. They thought I was anaemic but it turned out it was because I was drinking too much. It's something to do with the blood' (Sharon).

Tables 3.6, 3.7 and 3.8 illustrate how adolescents begin to assess the effects of drinking alcohol in terms of their positive and negative experiences. Most people in Britain, adults as well as teenagers, see moderate drinking as an acceptable, enjoyable and legitimate part of their leisure time and, indeed, young people's drinking cannot be understood without a consideration of adult society's use (and misuse) of alcohol. When young people start drinking in their early teens and they begin to learn how to drink, they experience the positive and sociable effects of the drug and balance these against the physical and emotional consequences of drinking too much. For the young people in this study, alcohol was associated with relaxation, enjoyment and disinhibition in social situations. These were balanced against the expense of alcohol, the hangovers, sickness and memory loss linked with over-indulgence, and also drink-related problems with friends, relatives and strangers. They learned both directly and through friends, relatives and elder siblings' experiences *how* to drink alcohol and the optimum levels of consumption for the desired degree of intoxication. This process of learning how to drink and how much to drink was evident when young people talked about their drinking in more detail in one-to-one interviews. For example, one

17-year-old interviewed who was asked what sorts of limits she put on her drinking said:

> I don't put any limit on in terms of units. I kind of know my limit, of how many wines or how many vodkas I've had. It's just a feeling really. Unless I've got to work the next morning or whatever and I know that I don't want to get drunk. I'd count them then.
>
> [In general what sort of limit would you put on your drinking?] Just until I don't want any more. I don't let it get to the sickness stage, I don't like that.

(Elaine)

One 17-year-old male respondent explained how he decided how much alcohol to have on a drinking occasion:

> What I do is like I'll drink and drink and drink, and then when I feel a bit ill I think well I think I should stop now. I'm not really conscious about how much I've drunk. It's just suddenly . . . hang on I'm drunk here or I'm going to be sick, so I stop drinking.

(John)

Similarly, a young woman explained the sorts of limits she put on her drinking in terms of gauging how she felt during the course of the drinking session rather than counting the numbers of drinks she consumed. 'I normally drink until I feel drunk and then I'll stop because once I feel drunk I don't particularly like to drink any more' (Vicky).

Young people's cost-benefit assessment evident here in their use of alcohol occurs for most young people well before their first experimentation with illicit drugs and, however uncomfortable this makes adult worlds feel, it is this approach to legal drugs which provides a framework for later decisions surrounding experimentation, continuation or cessation of illicit drugs made by the young people we interviewed.

Non-drinkers

And what of the small minority of young people who did not drink alcohol throughout their teens? At the age of 16, for example, twenty-six respondents had never had a whole alcoholic drink. When asked why they never drank alcohol, religion was the main reason given. Fifty-two per cent of 16-year-old abstainers said that it was because their religion forbids it. All except one were Muslim. Four in ten abstainers said alcohol is bad for one's health and four in ten said they did not agree with drinking alcohol for general reasons. Both parents and friends were influential on non-drinkers' decisions, with one-third (mainly Muslim) saying they did not drink alcohol because their parents disapproved and one-third saying they did not drink because their friends abstained too. Practical and legal considerations were less often reasons stated for not drinking: one-quarter did not like the taste of alcohol and 16 per cent of abstainers said they did not drink alcohol because they believed that it was against the law. By the age of 18, fifteen of the seventeen abstainers remaining in the sample were Muslims.

Smoking

The final section of this chapter concludes with details of survey results for tobacco, the second 'favourite' legal drug with our respondents. Tobacco use has been falling in Britain in all age groups from about half of the adult population over 16 in the 1970s to about one-third of over-16s in the mid 1990s. Research in the late 1990s, however, is suggesting young people's smoking rates are beginning to rise again, particularly amongst young women (Rowlands *et al.*, 1997). As with alcohol, the north and north-west of England have some of the highest levels of cigarette smoking, along with Scotland (Plant and Plant, 1992). Table 3.9 provides details of current smokers across the

Table 3.9 Five years' data on smoking cigarettes by gender (%)

		Current Smoker	*Non-smoker* [a]
Year 1	F	37.6	62.4
	M	22.2	77.8
Year 2	F	39.4	60.6
	M	25.1	74.9
Year 3	F	37.0	63.0
	M	27.9	72.1
Year 4	F	33.2	66.8
	F	33.2	66.8
Year 5	M	37.4	62.6
	M	37.4	62.6

Note:
a Non-smokers include those who have never smoked and those who no longer smoke

five years of this study. By the age of 18 one in four women and one in three men smoke cigarettes, despite the considerable health risks involved. In each year of the study young women are significantly more likely to smoke than young men.

Conclusion

The North-West Study provides evidence to reinforce and elaborate on earlier studies of adolescent drinking. In general young people start drinking alcohol in their early teens and most drink alcohol on a regular basis by their mid teens. During the adolescent years covered by this study we see evidence of the transition from home-based, parentally supervised, moderate and 'special occasions' drinking to experimental drinking in public places, parks and streets with friends, to socialising in licensed premises in the mid to late teens. From celebrating with relatives to socialising with friends, alcohol is an integral part of young people's leisure and pleasure in Britain in the 1990s. Considerable quantities of alcohol are consumed, with eight in ten of the respondents in this study drinking alcohol once a week or more by the age of 18 and with an average of nearly eleven units of alcohol being consumed per drinking occasion.

This study mirrors the trends identified in other studies of young people's drinking in the 1990s, covered earlier in this chapter, regarding increased sessional consumption, the popularity of high-strength ciders and lagers, and so on, suggesting our respondents are not untypical of young people in Britain in the mid 1990s. The fragmentation and diversification of the licensed trade, in part a response to declining business due to home drinking, eating out, dance club culture and alternative entertainments, has led to the development of a range of premises such as continental-style café bars, family friendly pub restaurants, theme pubs, 'fun' pubs, live music pubs and traditional pubs in the late 1990s. As the results of this study testify, although the form changes, the pub stays with us and remains a desirable place for modern youth to spend their 'time out' with their favourite drug.

From their early teens young people decide how much to drink and indeed whether or not to drink using a cost-benefit calculation which is part of their wider risk assessment regarding the repertoire of psycho-active substances to which they have access. Young people's cost-benefit calculations, whether conscious or not, involve weighing up alcohol (and possibly illicit drugs) and deciding whether the positive effects outweigh the negatives. By the age of 16 over nine in ten drinkers report having a good time and feeling happy after drinking. Conversely, at the same age about half of drinkers reported feeling unhappy after drinking, having had a 'hangover', been sick, and had a headache.

A decade after the Royal College of Psychiatrists' report (1986) alcohol remains 'our favourite drug', although in the mid 1990s it is complemented by or replaced by illicit drugs, such as cannabis in quieter social settings and the stimulant dance drugs like amphetamines and ecstasy in club settings, by growing numbers of young people. This study, as we shall see, confirms the links between heavier drinking and the use of tobacco, illicit drugs and other risk-taking behaviour. There is evidence from our interviews with young people of a blurring of the legal and illicit in their 'pick and mix' psycho-active culture with alcohol and tobacco acting as possible gateway drugs through to the illicit range, in a literal sense in that they usually precede experimentation with illicit drugs but more particularly because of the relationship between heavy and frequent drinking and drug use. Also of relevance to alcohol's possible gateway role is its physiological effect as a depressant or disinhibitor affecting or excusing young people's judgement, leading to alcohol being considered to be a cause of unplanned drug use for some of our respondents when they were intoxicated with alcohol. There is also evidence that some young people switch between psycho-active substances depending on desired effects, price, availability, social setting and so on, a subject we will scrutinise in later chapters.

As we have seen in this chapter, most young people learn to drink throughout their teens and it is an established part of their leisure-time socialising by the time they are old enough to drink legally in pubs and clubs. Neither victims nor delinquents, most young people drink because it is an enjoyable and acceptable part of their 'time out' from the stresses and pressures of their lives, a rational choice after weighing up the 'good times' and the 'bad times', a part of their celebrations with the family and their socialising with friends. Most young people enjoy their drinking but for a minority the frequency and severity of the negative effects associated with their drinking is, however, cause for concern.

4   Patterns

An overview of drug offers, trying, use and drugs experiences across adolescence

In this short chapter we provide an overview of the drug-related behaviour of our samples over the five years they were tracked from early adolescence into the beginnings of young adulthood. Essentially the findings, as laid out here, are typical of the way facts and figures about adolescent drug use in the UK are presented and published. Thus tables of drug offers, lifetime trying and more recent or regular use are presented. Nearly all the studies mentioned in Chapter 1, for instance, use this format and presentation style. The only obvious difference is that we are, uniquely, describing the situation based on the evidence of a five-year study which allows us to spot trends and see developmental change through time.

Drug offers and availability

Each year the young people in our samples were asked about whether they had been in situations where illicit drugs were available for free or to purchase. Even in Year 1 when our respondents were only 14 almost six in ten had been in such situations rising annually to over nine in ten in Year 5. Cannabis, as we can see from Table 4.1, is the drug most likely to be 'offered' or available, followed by amphetamines, LSD and, in later adolescence, ecstasy. Heroin and, to a lesser extent, tranquillisers and cocaine, remain the least accessible or available drugs for this particular generational cohort though this patterning seems likely to change amongst younger cohorts behind them (Parker *et al.*, 1998b).

Ever tried a drug

The statistic which inevitably becomes the headline figure when a survey of youthful drug use is published is the 'ever used' or lifetime prevalence rate. Table 4.2 describes these rates for our samples.

Table 4.1 Drug offers (age 14–18 inclusive)

	Year 1 (n = 776) %	Year 2 (n = 752) %	Year 3 (n = 523) %	Year 4 (n = 536) %	Year 5 (n = 529) %
Amphetamines	29.6	40.6	47.9	60.0	67.0
Amyl nitrite	24.1	37.3	41.7	51.4	58.9
Cannabis	54.6	61.6	72.7	77.4	83.9
Cocaine	8.0	12.7	12.4	19.4	23.7
Heroin	5.4	8.2	5.4	6.6	5.4
LSD	40.4	55.0	56.1	65.3	65.6
Magic mushrooms	24.5	32.5	29.2	26.9	26.2
Ecstasy	21.4	32.9	36.3	49.7	62.3
Solvents	25.6	27.2	23.1	33.7	27.3
Tranquillisers	4.3	11.4	7.1	12.8	14.4
At least one	59.1	70.9	76.5	87.5	91.1

We can see that self-reported drug trying rose from over one-third at the age of 14 through to almost two-thirds by the age of 18 years. This is a remarkably steep upward climb and is an important indicator of the degree of penetration of illicit drug trying amongst 1990s' adolescents. The most important epidemiological trend in this table involves 'incidence', that is first-time trying reports each year. As we can see, in late adolescence the incidence rate is actually picking up, a finding inconsistent with the notion of drug use as adolescent rebellion and thus slowing down, with maturation, by young adulthood.

We should remember, however, that lifetime trying rates are

Table 4.2 Lifetime prevalence of illicit drug taking (age 14–18 inclusive)

	Year 1 (n = 776) %	Year 2 (n = 752) %	Year 3 (n = 523) %	Year4 (n = 536) %	Year 5 (n = 529) %
At least one drug	36.3	47.3	50.7	57.3	64.3

primarily generated by annual re-reporting. Whilst two-thirds of the Year 5 sample had tried a drug, a vitally important finding, we must be very careful to emphasise that this figure will include those who tried a drug once or twice in early adolescence and those who have used drugs but have no intention of doing so again.

Ever tried, by specific drug

In Table 4.3 we redraw these lifetime rates by each of the main available illicit drugs. We can see quite clearly that cannabis dominates the drug trying of these young people, whereby the lifetime trying of cannabis is only slightly behind the overall 'at least one drug' lifetime trying rates. This said we can also see how by mid adolescence LSD and amphetamines will have been tried by over a quarter of the samples, closely followed by amyl nitrite 'poppers'. In late adolescence ecstasy trying also climbs rapidly whereby one in five will have imbibed their first tablet. Tranquillisers and heroin and, to a lesser extent, cocaine remain 'marginal' drugs with solvents and magic mushrooms, as early experimentation drugs, showing no incidence and indeed, as

Table 4.3 Lifetime prevalence of illicit drug taking (age 14–18 inclusive) by individual drug

	Year 1 (n = 776) %	Year 2 (n = 752) %	Year 3 (n = 523) %	Year 4 (n = 536) %	Year 5 (n = 529) %
Amphetamines	9.5	16.1	18.4	25.2	32.9
Amyl nitrite	14.2	22.1	23.5	31.3	35.3
Cannabis	31.7	41.5	45.3	53.7	59.0
Cocaine	1.4	4.0	2.5	4.5	5.9
Heroin	0.4	2.5	0.6	0.6	6.0
LSD	13.3	25.3	24.5	26.7	28.0
Magic mushrooms	9.9	12.4	9.8	9.5	8.5
Ecstasy	5.8	7.4	5.4	12.9	19.8
Solvents	11.9	13.2	9.9	10.3	9.5
Tranquillisers	1.2	4.7	1.5	3.9	4.5
At least one	36.3	47.3	50.7	57.3	64.3

discussed in Chapter 2, suffering from redefinition and under-reporting by Year 5.

First-time trying, by drug

At every stage of the study cannabis was the key drug tried by 'initiates': respondents who at each stage of the research were trying drugs for the first time. In early adolescence, perhaps because of their ease of availability, solvents, primarily gases and aerosols, were used and, as we can see, firmly rejected by older initiates. Nitrites (poppers) being illicit rather than illegal in the early 1990s, and fairly easily obtained, are, unsurprisingly, important for initiation. On the other hand LSD, a 'strong' Class A drug, is also a common first-experience drug. The very low cost of LSD as acid blotters or 'trips' and their ready availability will be relevant here. Ecstasy was not easily available to this sample's age group in the early 1990s and as we shall see ecstasy initiation is clearly age related in respect of access to dance clubs. The use of tranquillisers, heroin and cocaine as first-time drugs are for this age cohort fairly rare.

Recency of drug trying and drug use

It is vitally important to distinguish between those young people who have used one drug once or a few times only and those who become regular users of one or more drugs. We will make far more of these distinctions in the following chapter but in terms of a 'rough guide', Table 4.4 provides an initial overview.

Table 4.4 Prevalence of lifetime and more recent illicit drug taking (age 14–18 inclusive)

	Year 1 (n = 776) %	Year 2 (n = 752) %	Year 3 (n = 523) %	Year 4 (n = 536) %	Year 5 (n = 529) %
Lifetime	36.3	47.3	50.7	57.3	64.3
Past year	30.9	40.6	40.5	46.1	52.9
Past month	20.4	26.2	27.7	34.1	35.2
Past week	-	-	-	20.1	23.4

Asking young people when they last tried particular drugs is one way of identifying not just recency of drug use but also current, possibly regular, drug use. Respondents who indicate recent drug trying will include virtually all current regular users, as well as one-off triers, experimenters and initiators. Thus, while we do require more sophisticated measures than presented here to properly define current regular drug use, measures we work towards in Chapter 5, recency of use does provide one rough indication of current and regular drug use.

Nevertheless we can see that over half of the sample at Year 5 and over 40 per cent in the previous three years had taken a drug in the year prior to each survey. Whilst some of these will be 'initiates' most will not and here again is another indicator of the scale of the drug use amongst 1990s adolescents.

Past week use, a measure we introduced once our respondents were over 16 years, suggests that regular drug users make up between 20 and 25 per cent of our samples in late adolescence. We will concentrate on these drug *users* in later chapters.

The impact of gender, social class and race

In Table 4.5 we look at how gender, social class and race correlate with the basic measures of drug offers and drug trying. Remembering the caveats about the attrition of some working-class 'risk takers' and Asian abstainers, by Year 3 we can identify some significant changes in the profile of today's adolescent drug triers when compared with previous generations.

In keeping with the general trends identified in Chapter 1, we can see the closure of the gender gap in relation to drug trying. Whilst in the 1970s and 1980s we would find at least twice as many young men as young women trying drugs there are, in this study, few statistically significant differences. In line with their earlier maturation and 'older' friendship groups, young women were actually more likely to be in drug-offer and drug-trying situations in Year 1. This situation slowly reverses through mid adolescence and by the age of 17 we can see that young men are slightly more likely to be trying drugs and by Year 5 are more likely to be recent, possibly regular, users. This said, the key point to make is that well over half of the young women in this study have had illicit drugs and a significant minority take drugs repeatedly.

In respect of social class, we can see that early 'risk takers' who had tried a drug by the age of 14 were far more likely to come from 'working-class' catchment areas. This class difference slowly disperses

Table 4.5 Gender, class and race by offer and use statistics for at least one drug

	Total %	Female s%	Males %	Middle %	Working %	Black %	Asian %	White %	Other %
		Gender		*Class*		*Race*			
Year 1 (n)	(776)	(358)	(415)	(406)	(370)	(29)	(57)	(634)	(10)
Offer	59.1	64.5	54.2	55.4	63.2	72.4	26.3	61.0	60.0
Lifetime	36.3	37.7	35.2	30.8	42.4	44.8	14.0	37.5	40.0
Past year	30.9	32.7	29.4	25.1	37.3	41.4	7.0	32.0	40.0
Past month	20.4	21.8	19.3	15.3	25.9	31.0	3.5	21.0	40.0
Year 2 (n)	(752)	(362)	(384)	(426)	(326)	(27)	(50)	(636)	(8)
Offer	70.9	71.5	70.1	71.4	70.2	88.9	32.0	73.1	62.5
Lifetime	47.3	47.5	46.4	45.1	50.3	70.4	14.0	47.6	50.0
Past year	40.6	40.9	39.3	37.6	44.5	63.0	10.0	40.7	37.5
Past month	26.2	24.6	27.6	22.1	31.6	40.7	6.0	26.3	37.5
Year 3 (n)	(523)	(298)	(225)	(357)	(163)	(12)	(24)	(478)	(7)
Offer	76.5	76.2	76.9	75.6	79.1	75.0	54.2	77.8	71.4
Lifetime	50.7	49.3	52.4	47.9	57.1	75.0	16.7	51.7	57.1
Past year	40.5	38.3	43.6	38.7	44.8	66.7	4.2	41.6	57.1
Past month	27.7	24.5	32.0	24.9	33.7	66.7	4.2	27.8	42.9
Year 4 (n)	(536)	(302)	(233)	(364)	(172)	(9)	(30)	(491)	(5)
Offer	87.5	86.4	89.3	88.5	85.5	100.0	63.3	89.0	80.0
Lifetime	57.3	54.3	61.4	57.1	57.6	66.7	23.3	59.5	40.0
Past year	46.1	43.0	50.2	48.9	40.1	55.6	20.0	47.7	40.0
Past month	34.1	31.8	37.3	36.8	28.5	44.4	10.0	35.4	40.0
Year 5 (n)	(529)	(305)	(224)	(365)	(163)	(14)	(26)	(485)	(2)
Offer	91.1	90.8	91.5	91.8	89.6	100.0	73.1	91.8	100.0
Lifetime	64.3	62.0	67.4	64.1	64.4	71.4	38.5	65.4	50.0
Past year	52.9	49.2	58.0	54.0	50.3	57.1	26.9	54.2	50.0
Past month	35.2	28.2	44.6	36.2	32.5	42.9	15.4	36.1	0.0

with age and in late adolescence there is a strong sense of middle-class young people 'catching up'. Several other studies have produced similar findings in relation to social class. Again the key point to make is that social background is no longer a predictor or protector. Young people from all social backgrounds are now, broadly speaking, likely to try drugs during their adolescence.

As we explained in Chapter 2 the attrition in our sample has unfortunately made any statistical analysis of the impact of race unsafe after Year 3 (see Parker *et al.*, 1995). Up to that point we were able to show that Asians were considerably less likely to have ever had a drug than either young white or black respondents, but that there were no differences in rates of drug trying between black and white respondents. Whilst this statistically significant difference remained at Year 5 we reached this conclusion with only twenty-six Asian and fourteen black respondents in the sample (of 527) and little store should thus be put on this measure.

Experiences of drug trying

In Tables 4.6 and 4.7, although still concerned with overall patterns, we begin to demonstrate how a longitudinal study gives opportunities for more adventurous questioning and analysis. In Year 5 we felt able to ask fairly sophisticated questions about actual drug-taking experiences knowing they would be relevant to over half our sample and acceptable to the abstainers who had loyally stayed with the project. We concentrated on the most used drugs of cannabis, LSD, amphetamines and ecstasy.

Table 4.6 shows that feeling relaxed, friendly, happy and carefree were the most quoted positive experiences. Amphetamines and ecstasy scored highly in providing self confidence and particularly feeling excited, energetic, sexy and loving or caring. Cannabis was seen as the ideal drug to relax with.

Turning to the negative experiences reported on last occasion of drug use in Table 4.7, the primary finding is that overall very few negative experiences are reported, and this is particularly striking when compared with positive outcomes. Aside from headaches after any drug use and more significantly a sense of depression particularly after imbibing amphetamines and ecstasy, the rates of negative experiences were very low, routinely affecting less than one drug taker in ten.

Table 4.6 Respondents who reported positive experiences on last occasion of use for cannabis, LSD, amphetamines and ecstasy[a]

	Cannabis (n = 294) %	LSD (n =135) %	Amphetamines (n = 140) %	Ecstasy (n = 102) %
Last time I had [...] I felt ...				
part of a group	14.3	16.3	12.9	19.6
energetic	4.8	34.8	75.7	62.7
excited	6.5	34.1	42.1	47.1
friendly	43.2	31.9	45.7	58.8
carefree	33.0	28.1	25.7	35.3
relaxed	61.9	13.3	17.1	36.3
had fun	37.4	40.7	46.4	51.0
confident	12.2	14.1	28.6	42.2
loving/caring	12.2	3.7	15.0	33.3
sexy	4.4	5.2	12.9	38.2
strong	1.0	7.4	13.6	17.6
happy	33.7	34.8	35.0	51.0
in control	22.1	17.0	22.9	25.5
outgoing	13.9	18.5	23.6	29.4

The last time I had [...] as the effects were wearing off I felt ...

	(n = 292)	(n = 135)	(n = 141)	(n = 102)
relaxed	31.5	11.9	12.1	17.6
loving/caring	3.1	1.5	2.1	8.8
like having more	13.4	9.6	9.2	10.8
no problem	27.1	13.3	11.3	14.7
outgoing	1.7	1.5	0.0	3.9
sad it was over	4.8	15.6	14.9	19.6
friendly	7.2	10.4	6.4	7.8
happy	12.7	11.9	7.1	10.8
proud	0.7	1.5	0.7	0.0

Note:
[a] n's represent all those in the Year 5 sample who had provided detailed information on their last experience with each of the five drugs

Table 4.7 Respondents who reported negative experiences on last occasion of use for cannabis, LSD, amphetamines and ecstasy[a]

	Cannabis (n = 294) %	LSD (n = 135) %	Amphetamines (n = 140) %	Ecstasy (n = 102) %
Last time I had [...] I felt ...				
angry	1.0	2.2	0.7	1.0
out of control	1.4	14.8	4.3	9.8
worried about drug content	2.0	7.4	2.1	5.9
foolish	6.8	14.1	5.0	6.9
sad	1.4	2.2	1.4	1.0
lonely	0.7	3.7	2.9	0.0
anxious	2.4	19.3	7.1	7.8
scared	1.0	14.1	4.3	4.9
queasy	8.5	1.5	2.9	3.9
frustrated	2.0	5.2	2.1	1.0
paranoid	5.1	31.1	7.1	5.9
The last time I had [...] as the effects were wearing off I felt ...				
	(n = 292)	(n = 135)	(n = 141)	(n = 102)
depressed	5.8	21.5	29.8	23.5
headache	13.4	19.3	19.9	18.6
lonely	1.7	5.9	5.7	8.8
worried about drug content	1.4	3.0	2.8	5.9
afraid	1.0	1.5	5.0	2.0
disappointed	4.8	7.4	7.8	10.8
pain	0.7	0.7	3.5	1.0
worried	1.4	8.1	5.0	3.9
guilty	3.8	5.2	5.0	8.8
foolish	5.5	4.4	4.3	5.9
sick	9.6	6.7	17.0	13.7
glad it was over	4.5	16.3	2.8	6.9
paranoid	2.7	12.6	5.7	8.8

Note:
[a] n's represent all those in the Year 5 sample who had provided detailed information on their last experience with each of the five drugs

LSD shows up as the least predictable drug and the one most likely to trigger feelings of paranoia and anxiety whereby a minority of users were glad when the experience was over. Although relatively rare, 'bad trips' do, as we shall see in Chapter 6, have an important role to play, via drugs stories, in the cost-benefit assessment young drug contemplators usually make before deciding whether to try or retry a certain drug.

Conclusion

Whilst not nationally representative, the range of drug-use statistics presented in this chapter suggest that recreational drug use, dominated by cannabis and supported by LSD, poppers, amphetamines and, in late adolescence, ecstasy, has become widespread amongst ordinary British youth. Entering young adulthood, by the age of 18, almost all the young people in this study had been in drug-offer situations and over six in ten had tried an illicit drug. These early 1990s' rates, which are now being replicated in many other recent studies (e.g. Miller and Plant, 1996; Barnard *et al.*, 1996) are quite unprecedented. This level of penetration into youth culture has only been possible because of the increased propensity of young women and young people from all social backgrounds to try a drug. Being a female, middle-class, A-level student is no longer a protective drug-free profile. Once we ask recency-of-use questions it becomes clear that a significant minority of the sample, between one in four or five, probably use drugs fairly regularly, although, as we shall see, there are better ways of assessing this. This again is an unprecedented rate but clearly we are a long way off from saying that the majority of young people are illicit drug *users*.

On the other hand the increases in new triers, the rate of drug-trying incidence, shows no sign of slowing as this generational cohort moves into young adulthood. This epidemiological process combined with the fact that reported positive experiences of drug use far outweigh negative outcomes suggest drug trying and drug use are not transitory nor closely tied to the period of adolescence. These are all powerful indicators to be stored and assessed in the final chapter when we formally consider the notion of normalisation.

5 Pathways
Drug abstainers, former triers, current users and those in transition

The pathways analysis

Initial developments

In this chapter we break with the conventional approach to measuring and presenting the prevalence of illicit drug use. We move beyond the analysis presented in the last chapter of seeing prevalence as a dependent variable by simply comparing those who have tried a drug with those who haven't and attempt to provide a more multi-dimensional analysis. What have our samples, and core cohort in particular, been thinking and concluding about the use of drugs and how does this relate to their behaviour – if they *use* drugs, which drugs, how many drugs and how often? Basically we attempt to identify and distinguish those engaging in current, regular and sustained drug use from those who are not but might in the future and those who are not and have no intentions of ever trying illicit drugs. We call this a *drugs pathways* analysis. It provides a far more sophisticated understanding of young people's drug use than that described in Chapter 4.

As we built up a developmental picture of the samples' alcohol, tobacco and drug use and looked for characteristics or factors which correlated with and might explain particular profiles we began, implicitly at first but then explicitly, undertaking this drugs pathways analysis. Thus in Year 4 we began to test out our hunches that the sample were clustering around typical behavioural repertoires and decision-making processes in respect of alcohol, tobacco and illicit drugs. We used three separate questions to compute these pathway categories: the past drug use/recency question for the thirteen listed drugs; future intentions for drug use for the listed drugs; and a self-nominated four-option 'statement' question in which the respondents indicated that which best described their view of themselves, young people and drug use:

1   I take drugs myself. I think taking drugs is OK if you're careful and you know what you're doing.
2   I do not use drugs myself at the moment, but it is possible that I might in the future. I have no problem with other young people using drugs.
3   I do not use drugs myself and don't expect to. I have no problem with other young people using drugs.
4   I don't use drugs and I don't expect to. I don't think people should take drugs.

We then set about looking at whether the data supported our second outline hypothesis that there were two clearly distinctive pathways: *abstainers* and *current* (probably regular) *drug users* and another group in between. This third group in fact split empirically into *former triers* (or ex-users) and those *in transition*. The initial analysis that includes very detailed description of the reliability and validity issues was, as noted above, undertaken when our respondents were 17 (see Aldridge *et al.*, 1996). In this chapter, by also using Year 5 data, when respondents were 18 years old, we further develop the analysis. In particular we look at the core cohort (n = 223 including interviews with 86) who were with the study for the full five years and for whom we have complete data to build up the pathways retrospectively. Thus, we also look back from Year 5 to Year 1, attempting to identify key factors which have tended to affect or predict particular pathway journeys.

The construction of the drug status variables at 18

Abstainers were all those respondents who indicated never having tried *any* of the drugs in the list and who also indicated that they never *intended* to try any of the drugs. Abstainers nominated themselves into either the third or fourth of the four statement categories regarding themselves, young people and drug use.

The group of *former triers* comprised respondents who indicated having taken, often experimentally, at least one of the drugs in the list, but who simultaneously indicated that they intended never to take drugs again. Former triers or ex-users, nominated themselves into either the third or fourth statement categories regarding young people and drug use.

The group of *current drug users* comprised all those respondents who reported having had at least one drug, indicated that they might or would try again at least one drug in the list, and nominated themselves into the first of the four statement categories regarding themselves, young people and drug use ('I take drugs myself'). Finally, those *in transition* were respondents who indicated that they either would or might try drugs at some point in the future, either for the individual thirteen listed drugs or by nominating themselves into the second of the statement categories regarding young people and drug use, 'I don't take drugs myself at the moment, but it is possible that I might in the future.' The respondents in this group may or may not have already tried or used drugs as indicated in the past-drug-use/recency question. The rounded frequency distribution for this drug status pathway variable at Year 5 is shown in Figure 5.1.

The criteria for differentiating between abstainers and former triers from others in the sample are straightforward and the justification and face validity of the categories is transparent. The other drug-status categories, *current user*, and those *in transition*, however, require some investigation into the validity in terms of both the *prima facie* meaning and usefulness of these categories and the extent to which the respondents classified into these categories behave in ways we would consider predictable and definitive.

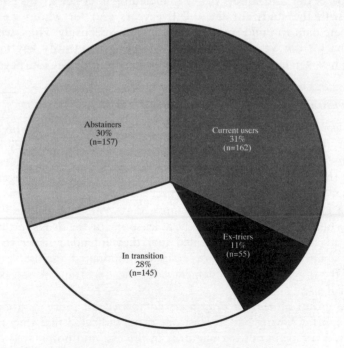

Figure 5.1 Drug status at age 18

Validation of current user categories

Of the various surveys of young people's drug use in Britain, none, so far as we are aware, has attempted to estimate prevalence rates of current drug users. Most have instead focused upon the estimation of drug-use prevalence rates based on *recency of use* measures (that is, how long ago the last occasion of usage occurred: within the past month, past year, or prior to the past year), similar to the one we have employed in each administration of the survey. Therefore, there is no available standard against which we can compare our estimate of prevalence rates of current drug users as a validation technique. Internal validity, however, can be addressed by exploring the responses to other questions answered by respondents in the current-drug-user pathway.

Current users are all those respondents who had ever tried a drug, intended to do so again and, crucially here, nominated themselves as drug users ('I take drugs myself'). This latter feature is key therefore in differentiating them from respondents *in transition* who had already tried a drug (who also intended future drug use but who did not nominate themselves as drug users). If this nomination is a valid way of differentiating current drug users from others who have tried a drug, then we should find key differences between these two groups, particularly on recency and frequency of drug use.

What 'usual' frequency of drug use most closely corresponds to the frequency that might be associated with the response 'I take drugs myself'? How often would someone use drugs in order to indicate agreement with this statement? Obviously, the criteria used to make this assessment will be different for each young person and will vary considerably also by drug taken, drug availability and could perhaps, for some respondents, even be unrelated to frequency of use at all. None the less, there is a common-sense validity in assigning a particular frequency to drug use that we should want to consider both regular and sustained, as well as current. A respondent whose usage is too infrequent is unlikely to qualify his or her usage as 'current'. We anticipated that 'less than once a month' would probably most likely correspond to occasional, non-regular, and possibly even non-current usage.

Respondents were asked to indicate the frequency of their past month usage for each of the drugs they had taken. For respondents in the current user group, the average past-month-use frequency for all drugs combined was 15.06, a figure substantially higher than that found among respondents in the transition pathway who had ever had a drug, who on average had done so less than once in the month prior to the survey (mean of .83). Clearly, then, the feature that distinguishes these two groups in terms of their construction (self-nominated drug user, 'I take drugs myself') also distinguishes between them in terms of their frequency of drug use: respondents who agreed with the statement 'I take drugs myself' on average had past-month-usage frequency that was more than 18 times that of the respondents in the transition pathway who had ever already taken a drug but had not agreed with the statement. Agreement with the statement thus has strong behavioural connections of the kind we would expect.

How accurate is our estimate that the current regular drug user is one who uses drugs at least, but probably more than, once a month? If our estimate of current regular use at a frequency of more than once a month is correct, then we should find that the majority of our current users had had a drug within the past month. In fact, we find that for 148 (91 per cent) of *current users* the most recent use of at least one drug occurred within the past month, compared to only eighteen (25 per cent) of respondents *in transition* who had ever had a drug. Furthermore among *current users*, fifty-one (32 per cent) had had a drug within the past week and sixty-four (40 per cent) either on the day they filled in the questionnaire, or the day before. Again, these comparisons show reassuringly marked differences in drug use behaviour when self-nominated drug status is taken into consideration.

Validation of the 'in-transition' category

The group we have identified as *in transition* (145, 28 per cent) is, unsurprisingly, much more diverse than the others in terms of respondents' drug-taking histories. Thirty-two (22 per cent) of respondents in this group have never had an illicit drug, though all of them either intended to do so, or thought that they might in the future. At the other end of the drug-use continuum, twenty-eight respondents *in transition* (about one in five of the group) had consumed a drug within the past month, but for the majority (19, 68 per cent) this occurred on only one or two occasions. The remaining twenty-six of the respondents who indicated more frequent usage had consumption levels ranging from three to twenty occasions within the past month. Does this suggest that this sub-group of frequent users *in transition* are respondents that we should consider *current users*, even if they themselves did not? If in fact they are similar to our group of self-identified *current users* in all but the self identification, we may wish to place less confidence in using self identification as a tool for classification.

In fact, however, if we compare the cluster of more frequent users *in transition*, who had used a drug more than once in the past month to the current users, we find they were much less likely than the *current user* group to have had a drug as recently as the past week and significantly less likely to have ever had amphetamines, nitrates, cocaine and ecstasy. These frequent in-transition users also had tried significantly fewer drugs in their lifetimes (mean of 2.7 compared to 4.4 for *current users*), as well as in the past year (1.8 compared to 3.2), past month (1.2 compared to 1.7), and past week (.25 compared to .98).

Similarly, the in transition group who had never tried a drug also differed significantly from the group to which they might reasonably be compared, the *abstainers*. For 'drug offers' the non-users in transition were significantly more likely to have been offered a drug than abstainers (94 per cent compared to 71 per cent of abstainers); and for specific drugs this difference in offer rates held true for amphetamines (59 per cent of non-users *in transition* compared to 35 per cent of *abstainers*); nitrates (50 per cent compared to 25 per cent); cannabis (88 per cent compared to 54 per cent); cocaine (19 per cent compared to 4 per cent); ecstasy (56 per cent compared to 37 per cent); anabolic steroids (13 per cent compared to 3 per cent); and tranquillisers (9 per cent compared to 3 per cent). Table 5.1 provides an overview of this analysis based on 521 respondents.

The drugs attitudes scale (DAS)

A further device was used both to validate the drug status pathways analysis and extend its analytic power. As well as comparing the drug use patterns for each pathway group we also created a drugs attitude measurement scale. Did each of our four pathway groups hold different attitudes about drug use and were these consistent with their self-reported behaviour?

Thirteen statements were devised in order to assess attitudes toward drugs and drug use:

1 Taking drugs is OK if it makes you feel good.
2 Taking drugs always leads to addiction.
3 I have a negative attitude towards drugs.
4 Taking drugs is always dangerous.
5 Most of my close friends take drugs.
6 People who take drugs live life to its fullest.
7 I could no longer respect someone who I found out took drugs.
8 Taking drugs is morally wrong.

Table 5.1 Drug-taking attitudes, behaviours and intentions for the Year 5 sample and by drug status

Drug status	Sample $(n=521)^a$ %	Current users $(n=164)$ %	Former triers/users $(n=55)$ %	In trans- ition $(n=145)$ %	Abstainers $(n=157)$ %
Drug-taking behaviour					
Recency					
Never	36.3	0.0	0.0	22.1	100.0
Prior to past year	11.1	0.0	67.3	14.5	0.0
Within past year	17.5	8.5	23.6	44.1	0.0
Within past month	11.7	20.7	9.1	15.2	0.0
Within past week	23.4	70.7	0.0	4.1	0.0
Number of listed drugs taken					
(drug triers only)	*(n=332)*				
Mean no. taken in lifetime	3.3	4.4	1.7	2.3	-
Mean no. taken in past year	2.1	3.2	0.4	1.3	-
Mean no. taken in past month	1.0	1.7	0.1	0.3	-
Mean no. taken in past week	0.5	1.0	0.0	0.1	-
Future drug-use intentions					
(excluding abstainers and former triers)	*(n=309)*				
Expecting to re/try at least one drug (excluding cannabis)	71.5	90.2	-	50.3	-
(excluding abstainers and former triers)	*(n=309)*				
Mean no. drugs expected to re/try	3.6	4.6	-	2.5	-
Attitudes	*(n=474)*				
Mean 'DAS' scores	37	47	35	37	29

Notes:
a Eight respondents with missing data could not be classified according to drug status

9 Older people worry too much about the dangers of drugs.
10 People who take drugs have mostly good experiences with drugs.
11 Cannabis should be made legal.
12 Taking drugs is just a bit of fun.
13 Most people who take drugs will eventually have problems.

For each of the statements, respondents were asked to indicate their level of agreement on a Likert-type scale that ranged from (1) 'agree strongly' to (5) 'disagree strongly'. Possible scores on the scale could therefore range from 13 to 65, with higher scores representing more 'pro-drug' attitudes. Actual scores ranged from 13 to 62, with a mean for the cohort of 37.26 (SD = 9.31).

A principal components factor analysis of the items in the scale confirmed evidence for the reliability and internal validity of the DAS as a uni-dimensional scale. One factor accounted for 43.7 per cent of the variance among items, and factor loadings for each item ranged from .51 to .79. A two-factor solution was neither empirically justified nor theoretically interpretable. The Cronbach's alpha coefficient was .89, indicating that the reliability for the scale was high.

Mean scores on the DAS between pathways were all in the expected direction. Thus, the *current users* had by far the highest pro-drug attitudes scores (mean 46.5) followed by respondents *in transition* (36.8), *former triers* (34.5) and *abstainers* (28.9). A one-way analysis of variance showed that differences in drug attitudes scores between groups were statistically significant, and post-hoc comparisons (Scheffe) showed that each group differed significantly from the others except for the small difference between former triers/users (34.5) and respondents in transition (36.8). And, providing further confirmation for the validity of the *in transition* group, we found that even the frequent drug users *in transition* (identified above) had significantly lower pro-drug attitudes (39.4) than the *current user* group (46.5). Similarly those in the *in transition* group who had never tried a drug had significantly more pro-drug attitudes (37.6) than *abstainers* (28.9).

In conclusion the drugs pathways analysis seems robust. Each pathway is measurably distinctive by attitude to illicit drugs, self-definition of drugs status and drug-taking behaviour (frequency, recency and number of drugs consumed). 'Future intentions', as we shall see when we compare pathways at Year 4 with Year 5, is a more complicated and necessarily elastic measure.

Drugs status groups

Abstainers

In the next chapter we look at the cost-benefit analysis which most drug users apply to assess whether they should take a particular drug. However, abstainers have also had to become drugwise during the 1990s and their critique of recreational drug use has its own sophistication and evolution. We did find a few 'classic' abstainers in our study who simply held the line:

> I've had it drummed into me even since I was little how bad it is and what it does to people. [Who by?] My mum and dad. Watch documentaries on it. I've seen how its affected friends. I've seen people get into debt. I think if you're the kind of person that can enjoy yourself you don't need it. I don't think anyone needs it. And, just the fact I'd be too scared. . . . I feel very strongly . . . I've never been tempted and I don't think I ever will be, or I know I never will be.
>
> [How do you feel about other people doing drugs?] It's upsetting that healthy people need to take things to give them a bit of a lift because its the effects afterwards.
>
> [Different views about different drugs?] I don't really know a lot about drugs. I know the different names but I don't actually know what each one does. But I know a drug's a drug and they're all bad.
>
> (Ellen)

However, such watertight perspectives, particularly from someone who pubbed and clubbed, were rare and whilst it is obviously possible to find an interview setting with mid-adolescents undergoing anti-drugs education whereby their views of those who take illegal drugs are wholly negative (Shiner and Newburn, 1996), such responses were atypical in this study. Why abstainers have had to become drugwise and how they are adapting to drug offers and drug use around them is an important plank in the normalisation thesis (Wibberley, 1997; Perry 6 *et al.*, 1997).

Abstainers are not usually risk takers and they readily admit that the thought of taking drugs scares them:

> [Why don't you take drugs?] They're expensive, I don't like injections. I don't like smoke as well. I don't like inhaling things. . . . I

don't want to damage my lungs, some people have reactions don't they just try it once and bang. . . . I'm scared about that as well. I wouldn't want to put myself in any situations. . . . I couldn't handle it.

(Samantha)

Because I'm scared really what they're going to do to me. I'm scared of not being in control and losing my mind and not knowing what I'm doing. It's just really my own personal choice – morals I suppose.

[Health?] Not really . . . I suppose it can kill you in the long run. I just don't think you need drugs to have a good time. I know people who can't go out without having Es.

(Josephine)

Yet both these outgoing and sociable abstainers did not regard their attitudes and moral perspectives as applicable to others. They felt each young person had to make up their own minds:

I feel quite strongly personally . . . but people should each make their own decisions especially where drugs are concerned.

[Different views on different drugs?] I think if you try pot I think that's OK but once you get into that circle that you've got contacts, the druggies, they think they can try other drugs, they start to experiment more and I think that's how it progresses.

(Samantha)

I used to think they were really stupid but now I think well if you want to do it, do it but don't encourage me to. The people that I hang around with *know* not to put them under my nose. . . . I hate seeing people off their faces . . . I feel really responsible if I'm with them.

[Different views about different drugs?] I think I'm calmer about Es and whizz and stuff like cannabis . . . rather than someone who's taking heroin or cocaine.

(Josephine)

These complex and coherent perspectives about the risks and dangers of taking illicit drugs were routinely found in the interviews with abstainers. They were clear about their self-prohibition but also acknowledged the 'right', however foolish, of their peers to take drugs. They judged drug users on the basis of how responsible their use of drugs was and which drugs they took. In short, they distinguished between responsible recreational drug use and a hard drug career: 'Everyone's got their own opinion. If they do take drugs then they're a bit daft but it doesn't bother me, like my cousin takes them [cannabis and amphetamines] and he's alright' (Tim). 'In a lot of ways I feel sorry for them. They've made a choice, its their problem. I just let them get on with it' (Paul).

One of the changes brought about by the widespread and early availability of illicit drugs in the 1990s is that abstainers cannot easily avoid social relationships with drug users. It is getting harder to change friends and peer groups and be insulated by like-minded peers and, thus far, more realistic to be upfront and accommodate difference:

> Only from a personal point of view I'd never do them, but as far as anyone else is concerned it doesn't bother me. Provided I don't get any pressure, it doesn't bother me.
>
> [And do you?] No not from the friends I've got.
>
> [Do they do drugs when you're out with them?] Yes.
>
> (Tony)

Such a strategy is not without its difficulties:

> [Have you ever felt awkward, upset about this?] I feel awkward sometimes when we're in a group and they say 'oh I'm going to get some drugs does anybody want some', I maybe feel isolated, not that I'd ever try, but I feel as if I'm not part of that group anymore, they then are in their own little group taking them as it were.
>
> [Do you feel pressured at all by that?] No, they may offer me, but they never pressure me. They say fine if you don't want any, fine.

However, there is a bottom line:

> It was a couple of years ago now really, one of my closest friends started taking drugs on a regular basis and I had to cancel a holiday with her and the friendship just split up really, I don't see her any more.
>
> [When you say you cancelled the holiday . . . was it because you just weren't to go with her because of it?] Not only that, but we were going with parents as well and they found out and they weren't very happy about it.

[Do you know what she was using?] She was taking speed, and I think she was taking ecstasy, but I can't be sure on that. She was smoking cannabis as well.

[Did you just gradually move away from her, or did you have a big bust up?] It happened gradually at first, at first I wasn't really bothered about it but her personality changed, she just changed completely into a different person, I just couldn't handle the change in her behaviour.

(Linda)

Overall abstainers having grown up with drugs and, having had to reject and negotiate so often around drug offers and drug taking situations, have themselves become drugwise. They feel that by and large, and certainly by late adolescence, their abstention is respected by triers and users and they in return come to accommodate soft drug recreational users not least because they might be a romantic partner, brother, sister or friend. This is, many of them feel, a sad and unfortunate state of affairs but it is a social reality with which they feel they must come to terms. Basically if you are outgoing and sociable and feel you have the right to enjoy yourself and party, pub, holiday in the sun or club without drugs then you must accept that others will behave differently. As one abstainer put it:

Drugs are always going to be there, no matter what you do about it, they'll always be there. Kids will always want to try them, and if they get away with it they'll try it again. If they've got the money they'll have it. And, to be honest there's nothing you can do about it. All you can do is to tell them how bad it is for them, and that's about it.

(Ben)

Former triers

The least crowded pathway is for former triers or ex-users. Whilst some have extensive drugs careers which they have now left behind most of this cluster have been experimenters or users only briefly. In some ways, for instance attitudinally, former triers are closer to abstainers. Similarly by declaring that they do not intend to try drugs again these former drug takers share an abstentionist perspective. However, behaviourally this pathway group have actually tried or indeed used illicit drugs and it is this experience which also brings them closer to drug users and those in transition who have also experimented.

One young man, a trainee accountant, who began using cannabis at 16 and then started using amphetamines alongside alcohol, changed pathways at 17. He continued to socialise in the same drug using group but had not taken an illicit drug for six months when interviewed:

> Basically it's [cannabis use] been part of our social life to have it every now and again. It mellows us out and puts us in good moods, that sort of thing. But it's not important to me at all and I can live without it. Like I say I haven't touched it for six months. . . . I suppose I've tried it all now. I know what it's like, rather than have the temptation being there for years and years.
>
> (Tom)

'Growing out of' adolescent drug use was seen by several interviewees as underpinning their giving up. One young woman continued to keep in the same peer network but stopped taking drugs (cannabis and amphetamines) several months before the interview. She put her decision to quit down to several factors: her mum finding out, feeling ill on several occasions, but most of all realising that she preferred drinking and clubbing. Looking back, her brief career was about:

> Just having a good time, everyone's doing it, so everyone's the same and there was nothing else to do when I did it with them and I was 14 to 16. There was nothing else to do . . . now because I'm older and can go to clubs and that.
>
> (Anne)

Several respondents in this pathway group only ever tried one drug on one occasion: 'It was weed. I had just a puff of one. That's all I had I didn't have the whole thing, just a puff. I was with friends and they were saying "go on just try it, try it" . . . I really hated it. I never touched it again' (Alice).

A final key definer for ex-users and triers was that many gave up because of a bad or very bad drug experience, often with LSD or, in the case of our most salutary account, 'tablets' purporting to be MDMA. When he was 16 one of our now ex-user interviewees went clubbing with his girlfriend. They bought tablets in the club. He took one and his girlfriend took two: 'My girlfriend, she just dehydrated, just collapsed. She was drinking beer, and you know beer, it doesn't actually quench your thirst does it? She just collapsed' (Daniel).

This young woman died several days later and our interviewee has not taken an illicit drug since, although he now drinks heavily.

In transition

Conceptually this pathway is the most difficult to define. Because this cluster are reviewing and revising their drugs status there is a sense in which they are on a roundabout rather than taking a clearly signed route. At Year 4, three-quarters of the in transition group had tried a drug and felt they might do so again in the future. The other quarter had no direct personal drugs experience but felt they might want to try a drug in the future. As we shall see, over half of this group actually change status and move down another pathway during Year 5 thereby giving further justification for this conceptualisation. We should also remember that this cluster, [although clear they were drug *users*] had fairly pro-drug attitudes and this in particular distinguished them from the abstainers. Thus one young man in transition, a keen sportsman, committed to a healthy lifestyle, was happy to have a friendship network of drug users despite the fact he'd never tried an illicit drug himself. Asked if he had any strong feelings about drug use he replied: 'No, not bothered at all. I've no thoughts about it whatsoever, no feelings.'

This interviewee made a clear distinction between 'soft' drugs and 'hard' drug use. He had no truck with junkies but felt cannabis was benign. Asked about his future intentions: 'Maybe . . . depends what mood I'm in. Depends how much I'd had to drink. [Situation?] Who I'm with I suppose. [Which drugs?] Cannabis only' (Craig).

An 18-year-old female, keen on sport, who had tried cannabis, LSD and magic mushrooms did not regard herself as a drug *user* because she settled for occasional binges of combination drug use involving alcohol, cigarettes and cannabis. She again felt comfortable with this status within her peer network. Typical of those in transition who used drugs she did so less often than current users: 'Usually do it when it's available, they're there, and they just say "do you want to try it" or "do you want to today?" and I just say yes or no' (Sophie).

Anther non-trier who'd used the cost-benefit assessment and decided against drug trying felt she was becoming increasingly agnostic through time:

> I don't really feel strongly about it, it's just up to now I've chosen not to. Like I said before, each to their own, it doesn't really bother me. . . . I feel more strongly towards say ecstasy or cocaine or heroin. I'm more against them.
> [In the future?] Yes I could do.
> [Situation?] Either with family or friends.

[What might influence your decision?] Just the consequences really.

[Which drugs?] Cannabis . . . I'm a bit indecisive about these hallucinogenic drugs cos I think they're a bit too dangerous for my own liking.

(Alison)

A 'big drinking' male interviewee felt similarly:

When I was younger it was very important, because it was sort of like being clean if you know what I mean. You haven't had nothing so you're clean. Getting older, it's not as important now, as I said . . . I'm tending to go that way a bit now as if I want to try something, but I haven't decided yet.

(Ben)

Moving into adulthood and going to university or having access to the nightclub scene was identified by several in transition interviewees as being a likely change in set and setting which might well stimulate their drugs initiation or diversification into dance drugs. One young man who was beginning to experiment with amphetamines could see his first E around the corner:

Just to experiment really. That's it. Just to experiment, just to try them. I suppose the atmosphere of clubs makes me want to try them . . . not really because my friends are doing it, it's because I want to experiment myself. I mean, my friends never ever pressure me at all, no peer group pressure at all, its basically my choice.

(Lee)

Current drug users

The next chapter is dedicated to describing journeys through adolescence which result in young people becoming drug users and here we shall only briefly outline this pathway group. We have shown that current users hold the strongest pro-drug attitudes and many speak with some disdain at the hypocrisy of alcohol- and tobacco-loving adults *vis à vis* cannabis and the way anti-drugs campaigns include cannabis as a 'drug of death':

I think it's sad really that people are so concerned about pot, a harmless drug. I say harmless, I'll take it for granted that its harmless, for the moment because as far as everybody knows it is, apart from the tobacco in it. When there are so many things that people should do something about . . . all the funds that go into . . . can you imagine all these thousands of people working making leaflets against cannabis, how sad is that.

(Ricky)

Drug users take far more drugs more often than those in transition and demonstrate they have learnt to distinguish between drugs and their effects.

Favourite combination, yes, speed, cannabis and alcohol. It's all three in all kinds of situations.
[Order?] Probably have a drink first and then it'll be the speed and then a lot later on we'll probably have the cannabis.

(Vicky)

And they enjoy their drug use and as we shall see have far more good times than bad:

You're in a really good mood, its more inside, nobody can annoy you no matter how gorgeous or how skinny the girl that stands next to you, it just doesn't really bother you, you feel like you're the nicest person in there. It gives you confidence.

(Diane)

[Where do you usually take drugs if you do?] Mainly in a night-club. Or, there was a phase we went through . . . there's like a brook near a waterfall, and a waterfall sounds dead peaceful at night time, and there's this big concrete slab, and about eight, nine of us used to go up there and we used to sit and have a spliff, and it used to be dead relaxing. A friend of mine got a jungle tape and it was really relaxed and there was like soul breaks in it, and we put that on these speakers you get with a Walkman, and sat there looking at the waterfall mist and looking at the stars, and everyone's just like falling asleep. It's wicked. Just lay there. Such a warm night, we just sat there smoking, just really chilled out, relaxed.

(Gary)

Those taking the drug-using pathway expect to continue to take or try drugs in the future but also to modify or restrain their behaviour.

[You haven't used LSD for a couple of years now . . . ?] Yes, I think I've matured with drug use. At first I was into trying anything, now I know what I like, what I don't like. I don't particularly like taking amphetamine, the after effects, but when you're on it it's alright. I probably will give that up, and probably, I've not taken LSD for a long time, but if I do take it again I'll probably just take one tab just for old time's sake. But with weed I wouldn't mind carrying that on. I don't know if I definitely will or not, but I'd like to.

(Adam)

This early risk taker who left school at 16 in the midst of a heavy poly-drug period also reminds us that his peers are joining the current users pathways just as he is restraining his use:

I would say a lot more [of them] are into it now. When I started I was young, it seemed mad to others of my age but once we left school they were also using drugs whereas they had criticised me in the past. Seems they have now caught up.

(Scott)

Others leaving sixth form and setting off for college, expecting new adventures, thereby remind us that here is another dynamic, undulating drugs pathway:

I think it'll all change when I go to Uni. I'll go to a lot more clubs hopefully.
[Which drugs do you plan to use in the future?] Whizz, more whizz. Probably weed will stay the same.
[Anything else?] No that's about it.
[More or less often?] More often.
[Amounts?] Probably increase but I won't try anything new now, I'll stick to what I know.

(Kate)

The making of drug pathways

In this section we take the drugs status of our core cohort at Year 5, as they enter young adulthood and look back down the pathways from which they've come from when they were 13 and 14 years old. In short we analyse what factors, decisions and behaviours in early and mid adolescence correlate and predict drugs status at Year 5.

First drug offers and first drug trying

It is quite clear from Tables 5.2 and 5.3 that there were situations, actions and decisions back in early and mid adolescence which helped shape the particular pathway journeys taken. We can see that *abstainers* were least likely to be in drug-offer situations in early and mid adolescence although as time went on they too nearly all encountered such situations. However even at 13–14 years of age nearly three-quarters of *current users* had already been in such situations. *Former triers* and ex-users as we can see are a small but more complex cluster. Some were in fact early risk takers who were both in offer situations at 14 and had also, by then, tried their first drug (34.8 per cent). We also find that at around 18 years of age (Year 5) another significant minority became abstinent and declared themselves as *ex-users* and former experimenters. The *in transition* cluster consistently take the middle course and were more likely to be in offer situations than *abstainers* and obviously by definition more likely to have tried a drug. There is an incremental steadiness about their initiation over the five years. *Current users* however clearly have the longest drugs careers, nearly half having already tried a drug at 14 and nearly all the remainder initiating by 17.

Table 5.2 Year in which respondents first reported being in a drug-offer situation for any drug for the cohort and by drug status at Year 5

			Drug-status Category			
	Cohort *(n = 223)*		*Current users* *(n = 64)*	*Former triers* *(n = 23)*	*In transition* *(n = 64)*	*Abstainers* *(n = 72)*
	n	*%*	*%*	*%*	*%*	*%*
Offer situation never reported	10	0.0	0.0	0.0	0.0	0.0
Offer situation of any drug first reported						
Year 1	121	54.3	73.4	65.2	53.1	34.7
Year 2	38	17.0	12.5	8.7	29.7	12.5
Year 3	21	9.4	12.5	8.7	4.7	11.1
Year 4	23	10.3	1.6	8.7	7.8	20.8
Year 5	10	4.5	0.0	8.7	4.7	6.9

Table 5.3 Year in which drug use first reported for the cohort and by drug
status

	Cohort (n = 139)ᵃ		Drug-status category		
	n	%	Current users (n = 64) %	Former triers (n = 23) %	In transition (n = 52) %
Use first reported					
Year 1	55	39.6	46.9	34.8	32.7
Year 2	23	16.5	18.8	17.4	16.5
Year 3	17	12.2	17.2	8.7	12.2
Year 4	26	18.7	15.6	8.7	18.7
Year 5	18	12.9	1.6	30.4	12.9

Note:
ᵃ only respondents in the cohort who have never had a drug included. Never reported
n = 84

Smoking and drinking by pathway status

The discovery that *current users*, at 18–19 years of age, had been far
more likely to have begun smoking tobacco in early adolescence and to
have sustained and indeed increased this consumption pattern through
into young adulthood is highly significant both statistically (see Tables
5.4 and 5.5) and epidemiologically. *Abstainers* by contrast demonstrate
that not smoking is another important related decision they make.
Over two thirds of *abstainers* have never smoked and only a tiny
minority have ever been regular smokers (see Table 5.4). Once again
the *in transition* group sit very close to the mean, taking the middle
ground, being more likely to smoke than *abstainers* and *former triers*
but far less likely than *current drug users*.

Drinking is far more normative than smoking in the UK and the
majority of all young adult Britons drink every week. We must thus
expect most *abstainers* in any representative sample to indulge in
drinking. This is in fact the case with over two thirds beginning drinking
around 14 and only 22 per cent never engaging in weekly drinking (see
Table 5.5). This said, *abstainers* reach their weekly drinking far later
than all the other pathway groups. Again the *former triers* group appear

Table 5.4 Smoking status for the cohort at each year and by drug status

	Cohort (n = 223) %		Current users (n = 64) %	Former triers (n = 23) %	In transition (n = 64) %	Abstainers (n = 72) %
			Drug-status category			
Year 1 (n = 214)						
Ever smoked	71	33.2	57.4	26.1	34.4	13.0***
Current smoker	41	19.2	37.7	8.7	16.4	8.7***
Year 2						
Ever smoked	116	52.3	77.8	52.2	57.8	25.0***
Current smoker	55	24.8	50.8	21.7	20.3	6.9***
Year 3						
Ever smoked	129	58.1	85.9	56.5	65.1	27.8***
Current smoker	64	288	59.4	26.1	23.8	6.9***
Year 4						
Ever smoked	142	63.7	92.2	69.6	73.4	27.8***
Current smoker	61	27.4	62.5	30.4	18.8	2.8***
Mean no. smoked yesterday	53	8	9	9	8	5 n.s.
Year 5						
Ever smoked	150	67.3	93.8	73.9	78.1	31.9***
Current smoker	85	38.1	81.3	43.5	32.8	2.8***
Mean no. smoked yesterday	66	11	11	8	12	0 n.s.

Note:
p≤.001

to contain some early risk takers, a third (34.8 per cent) who begin weekly drinking in early adolescence, and another cluster who begin regular drinking at around 17 when access to pubs and age presentation at off licences made social drinking accessible. *Current users*, with the exception of a couple of respondents who don't like or drink alcohol, were already drinkers by 14–15 years of age and three-quarters were weekly drinkers by 16.

Table 5.5 Drinking status for the cohort at each year and by drug status

			Drug-status category			
	Cohort *(n = 223)* *n*	*%*	*Current users (n = 64)* *%*	*Former triers (n = 23)* *%*	*In transition (n = 64)* *%*	*Abstainers (n = 72)* *%*
Current drinking never reported	7	3.1	1.6	0.0	0.0	8.3[a]
Current drinking first reported						
Year 1	187	83.9	95.3	87.0	89.1	68.1
Year 2	17	7.6	3.1	8.7	7.8	11.1
Year 3	9	4.0	0.0	4.3	1.6	9.7
Year 4	1	0.4	0.0	0.0	0.0	1.4
Year 5	2	0.9	0.0	0.0	1.6	1.4
Weekly drinking never reported	21	9.4	1.6	4.3	4.7	22.2[b]
Weekly drinking first reported						
Year 1	49	22.0	26.6	34.8	25.0	11.1
Year 2	49	22.0	32.8	8.7	25.0	13.9
Year 3	40	17.9	15.6	13.0	20.3	19.4
Year 4	42	18.8	18.8	34.8	12.5	19.4
Year 5	22	9.9	4.7	4.3	12.5	13.9

Note:
[a] = $p \leqslant .05$; [b] = $p \leqslant .001$

Risk-taking indicators

This same patterning by pathway group holds for all the other 'deviance' or risk-taking indicators utilised in the study. For early sexual experiences (more than a kiss!) under the age of 16, abstainers were far less likely than current users to have had a sexual experience (p<.001). At 16, 76 per cent of abstainers reported not having had sex but only 41 per cent of current users did so (p< .01). Former triers (61 per cent) and those in transition (53 per cent) were also less likely to have had under-age sex than current users (see Newcombe *et al.*, 1994).

Exactly the same patterning occurs when we look at our cohort's involvement with the police and criminal justice system. At Year 5 just under half (46 per cent) of the cohort had been stopped by the police including 72 per cent of current users. However 81 per cent of abstainers had still never been stopped by the police (p<.001). Statistical significance remains between these two contrasting pathways for being arrested (p<.01) and being cautioned or convicted (p<.01).

However, whilst all this shows defining differences between users and abstainers it should not detract from the other vitally important conclusion – that despite the war-on-drugs rhetoric about the link between drug use and crime, hardly any of the cohort are seriously delinquent and over two-thirds (67 per cent) of current users have no cautions or convictions either. Moreover, just being out and about increases one's risk of being stopped and arrested.

Drugs pathways into young adulthood

In this section we identify and discuss the continuity and change in the cohort's drugs status between Years 4 and 5. The period coincided with the cohort having an 18th birthday and obtaining many of the official trappings of adulthood. For many it was a time for leaving home and going to college or university, for others jobs and wages kicked in.

Abstainers

Figure 5.2 illustrates the longitudinal changes in the abstainer cluster. One abstainer became a current user whilst a handful became former triers by briefly experimenting with drugs during Year 5. Two of the fourteen in this category tried only one drug before quickly returning to abstention as former triers. In Year 5, 16 per cent moved into transition; half of whom only made an attitudinal change by declaring that

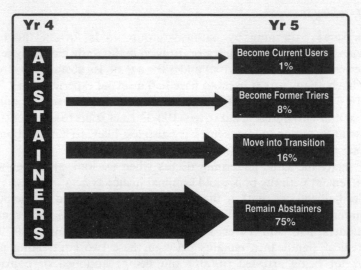

Figure 5.2 Pathways for abstainers between Year 4 and Year 5

it was now a possibility they would take a drug in the future. The remainder actually tried one, usually two, drugs during Year 5 and acknowledged they would probably do so again, thereby further confirming their shift out of abstention.

All this said, 75 per cent of this pathway group who had never taken a drug during their whole adolescence maintained this position on into young adulthood. Whilst there are clearly grounds for believing the abstainer group will further diminish in size, it is also very likely that the majority of these abstainers will sustain their status.

Former triers

Former triers and ex-users are a small proportion of the cohort but as we can see from Figure 5.3 they continue to review and redefine their status. During Year 5, 43 per cent continued as *former triers* and if we include the four respondents who were anomalous reporters by 'forgetting' at Year 5 if they had once tried a drug (as discussed in Chapter 2) then over half have remained on the same pathway.

This said the remainder have moved back towards drugs with 11 per cent becoming *current users* and no less than 38 per cent moving into *transition*. Of the eighteen in this latter pathway half had used a drug, primarily cannabis, very recently. The remainder had only made the

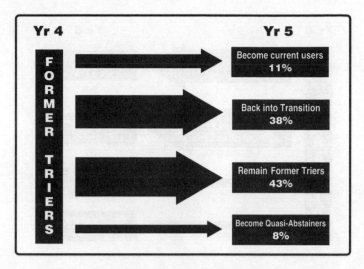

Figure 5.3 Pathways for former triers between Year 4 and Year 5

intellectual or attitudinal shift by declaring that they might take another drug in the future. Overall, in terms of actually imbibing a drug during Year 5 only thirteen of these forty-seven *former triers* actually indulged.

In transition

By definition we should expect considerable movement in the in transition cluster. Figure 5.4 confirms this. No less than fifty (37 per cent) of the cluster became *current users*. This is a substantive shift because it involves a major behavioural change. Most of these new *current users* (44, 88 per cent) had already tried a drug. Primarily what we have measured is the operationalising of their intentions several months before. Having taken one or more drugs in the past and expecting to do so in the future this group then quickly moved into a level of drug use which defined them as *current users*. Nine respondents became *former triers* and nine became *abstainers* during Year 5 sharing a shift away from drugs. For the half (49 per cent) that remained *in transition* two-thirds (45) had already had a drug. Overall therefore we must accept that the majority of those who take the in transition pathway are more likely to move towards rather than away from regular drug use.

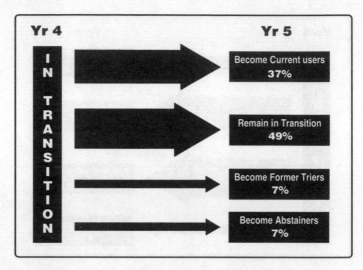

Figure 5.4 Pathways for those in transition between Year 4 and Year 5

Current users

This pathway group (n = 164) have undertaken the least change *vis à vis* drugs (see Figure 5.5). No less than 80 per cent remain *current users* by attitude, future expectations and drug-taking behaviour during Year 5. With only two respondents giving up drug use to become ex-users, the only other shift was for the 16 per cent who moved 'back' into transition by no longer agreeing with the statement 'I take drugs myself.' This does not mean they no longer ever take drugs. In fact half were past-month users of cannabis. We are here probably measuring a reduction in frequency and range of drugs used that many feel inconsistent with defining themselves 'drug users'.

Summary

We have shown how the four discrete drugs pathways our samples have taken during their adolescence are conceptually robust. The *abstainer*, *former trier*, *in transition* and *current user* pathways are identifiable by attitude, future expectations about drug use and actual drug trying and drug taking behaviour. *Abstainers* hold anti-drugs attitudes, have never taken a drug and never intend to. *Former triers* and ex-users hold fairly negative attitudes to drug use and whilst they have tried or used

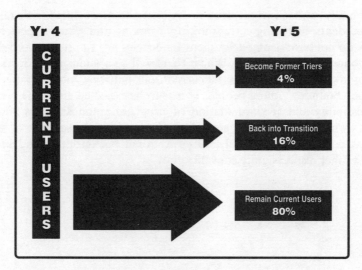

Figure 5.5 Pathways for current users between Year 4 and Year 5

illicit drugs during their adolescence they have no intention of doing so again. Those *in transition* hold fairly positive drugs attitudes, most have tried drugs but, importantly, all feel they might use drugs in the future. *Current users* hold pro-drug attitudes, they use one or more drugs regularly and expect their drugs careers to continue into the future.

Whilst each of these pathways are 'static', young people by reflecting on and reviewing their attitude to and use of drugs can switch pathways. We have shown by plotting young people's decision-making journeys that as our samples move into adulthood there is a continuing increase in the proportion who are becoming *current users* and a reduction in the number of *abstainers*. Most young people who become drug users move gradually into regular drug use and so spend periods in transition.

All this is complicated by the fact that today's youth distinguish between different drugs in a fairly sophisticated way whereby those *in transition* for instance are more likely to use the 'softer' drugs such as cannabis whereas *current users* have a larger, often combination, drug repertoire including amphetamines and ecstasy. *Abstainers*, particularly in late adolescence, also accommodate those who are 'sensible' recreational users of 'soft drugs' thereby also showing drug wisdom consistent with the normalisation thesis.

Finally, whilst current drug users have the most florid, risk-taking antecedents, including early smoking, drinking and sexual experiences, they do not have strong delinquent tendencies nor fit into any typology of abnormal development. Whilst there will be a minority of drinking, drug taking delinquents in the *current user* pathway, most are conventional 'bounded' young people. This is to be expected given the greater accessibility and accommodation of drug use amongst 1990s adolescents whereby, as we have seen, today's young drug users are of both sexes, come from all social and educational backgrounds and are in most other respects quite conventional.

6 Journeys

Becoming users of drugs

Introduction

In this chapter we offer little further quantification. Instead we describe and illustrate the 'journeys' which young people make as they try certain drugs and weigh up whether a particular drug can or will, on balance, be used more regularly. In making these experimental, sometimes existential, journeys drug triers and users become far more *drugwise* as they make and remake what are clearly identifiable *cost-benefit assessments* about regular drug use.

We have already seen that committed abstainers hold distinctive attitudes and expectations about illicit drug use which 'protect' them from this journey although they are often interested and concerned onlookers. Here we focus on those who have tried or use drugs. We rely heavily on their oral histories given at around 17 and 18 years of age. Their drugs journeys are of course tied up in the general pace and drama of adolescence as they face up to educational challenges, career decisions, mutating friendships, sex, romance and a changing relationship with parents. Being *drugwise* is one of the extra responsibilities which 1990s' adolescents face because they must grow up in a world in which drugs are an everyday reality.

We listen to young voices actually describing how they get their drugs, what actually happened the first time and how they assess risk before trying again. As we have already seen in respect of alcohol, risk assessment is part of the cost-benefit calculation and it involves weighing up for each drug the likelihood of bad or frightening experiences, the health risks, and the impact of 'getting caught' by teachers, parents, employers or the police. These are weighed against the pleasure and enjoyment of particular drugs and their ability either to blank out stress and distress or most often help deliver cost effective, deserved 'time out' through relaxation and enjoyment from the grind of ordinary, everyday life.

This drugs wisdom, the knowledge basis, is of course far from complete and rarely wholly accurate. Indeed as we shall see there are many versions of 'the truth' as each young person attempts to compute their own position from the plethora of often contradictory information they receive from friends, schools, parents and the media. One significant process in all this is the role of drugs stories – community 'folk tales' about what has happened to drug-trying young people locally. These tales are microcosms of the 'global' stories presented by the media. They are told and retold to support the views and perspectives of the raconteur. Thus stories about people being excluded from school, 'tripping' on the college bus or being hospitalised after an excessive night of clubbing on drink and drugs all become important contemporary folk tales.

Getting drugs

Drugs availability

In early adolescence those young people we have called 'risk takers' are far more likely to have been in situations where drugs were available. Thus we find our early drug takers have many more stories about being in these situations, even at school:

> There used to be open dealing in the corridors. You could shout out and ask if anyone had any trips and several people would say 'yeah I've got some'.
>
> (Year 5, joint interview, two female poly drug users)

Quite often availability and initiation were combined, as in this situation when one interviewee looked back on being 14 and being given her first drug (LSD):

> Acid, strawberry.
> [Who were you with?] At a school concert, I was with my mates about twenty of them . . . one of my mates in school he had to ask his cousin.
> [What did you think?] It took about two hours before I noticed anything then I was dead aware of everything.
>
> (Claire)

However by mid adolescence, around 15 and 16, these situations were encountered by the majority of our respondents rather than just early drugwise experimenters and users: 'We used to go to a Teens Scene, and at the end of GCSEs we all went down to the beach and there was plenty of them around there' (Sandra, poly drug user).

By late adolescence most respondents and interviewees had been in a whole range of situations where drugs were available and talked about:

They were always available with the people I knew from school. And some bloke on the train offered me some for free.

[What did you say?] I told him I didn't really want any.

[Anywhere else?] Parties I suppose . . . just being passed around . . . pot, acid, really anything.

(Martin, cannabis only trier)

Yes . . . in any number of places – pub, the park, at school, just generally around, street corners. They don't have to be friends, they're not really dealers either, they're sort of friends of a friend of a dealer and it all gets passed down. I don't really think there's any proper dealers [around here].

(John, cannabis user).

Pubs, clubs, on the street, parties. That's about it really.

[Friends?] Friends, well not close friends but people you know through people you know.

[What drugs?] Es, LSD, speed, cannabis.

(Ian, non-user)

Pubs, friends' houses.

[Dealer friends?] Well yes for free and then dealers. If you see people you know and you say 'alright' they just say 'Oh I've got this, you can have some.'

[Who's offering the drugs generally?] Mainly friends, but a few people I know they deal and that, so they've offered.

[For money?] Sometimes, if it's a dealer it's for money but if it's a friend they'll say, just have a bit . . . just weed. I can have weed on tick. Whizz, and I've been offered trips and things like that for free, but nothing like that interests me.

(Karen, cannabis user)

Yes loads of times *The Scream* and one time we were in *Trios* in town, we got offered tablets twice, by the same fella, you know asking again. . . . Oh and at *Pandora's* one time. That was speed.

(Amy, trier, non-user)

Friends as dealers

In these everyday worlds we are penetrating, a far more blurred line between user and 'dealer' emerges than 'war on drugs' discourse discussed in Chapter 1 could contemplate. Whilst our interviewees (n = 86) had been offered drugs by dealers and strangers, the majority of their experiences of being in drug offer situations were related to friends, acquaintances and friends of friends:

I've got two sets of friends and I take them [cannabis] with both. With this [town] having a beach it's either down the beach or in this friend's house that I was telling you about before.
[Where do you get your stuff?] I know some guy at school who can get it, although he's not a dealer he knows someone who's not a dealer who can get it.
[Reliable quality?] The quality's not bad but getting it's a pain in the arse quite frankly . . . I never think I'll be able to get it in time and if I do I think it'll be rubbish stuff, until I'm stoned, then I realise that it's not actually that bad.
[How far in advance do you get it?] Usually it's oh I'll get draw for next week, ask around and people say oh I can get it you by Friday.

(John)

My friend's house, her boyfriend sells pot but if he's got any spare he'll pass it round, don't have to pay, or sometimes we'll pay for it.

(Lisa, poly drug user)

Most drug users were as likely to have drugs 'for free' as purchased, thus again blurring the dealer–user line whereby some drugs have become seen, like cigarettes, as symbolic signs of friendship to be given freely. For his 18th birthday one male regular user who usually paid for his drugs was told by one of his friends: 'it's your birthday if you want we'll club together and get some drugs for you' (Martin).

One interviewee, a cannabis user at 17, noted how younger children saw her, because she was a drug user, as a potential source of drugs.

I've had little kids ask me. A few lads about twelve asked me to go and get them something [cannabis] and I just said no. Because I think its wrong at that age.

[Would other people get stuff for them?] A few of my mates, drugs yes, and, ale as well. I know people who go and get them ale.

(Karen)

Whilst refusing to get drugs 'for children' is one thing, a significant minority of drug users in our samples had obtained drugs for other friends, usually 'for free', sometimes with 'clubbed together' resources and sometimes to cover the costs of their own drugs bill. One experienced poly drug user whose parents accepted her lifestyle ran a fairly extensive supply system for friends and particularly 'friends of friends'. Whilst this began as: 'I'm normally the stupid one who sorts everything out for everyone.' It soon became a well-organised process.

[How often do you sort people?] Weekly. Depends what's going on, if there's any special occasions . . . for other people I've got whizz, Es, trips.

This young woman also worked out that having cannabis around, to sell, carried other risks:

I used to do quite a bit of dealing, but it just meant that I'd smoke more, I used to smoke it [supplies] before I'd sell it, so it wasn't a good system.

(Louise)

We interviewed one young man whose dealing moved beyond the home and acquaintances into a local nightclub. His situation reminds us how, for a minority, drugs careers and delinquent careers can intertwine. He and a friend working as bar staff came to an arrangement with door staff whereby they sold amphetamines, LSD and ecstasy: 'some nights we were walking out with about £600 in our pockets. It wasn't bad but things started getting heavy when CID came in'.

It was not just police interest that dissuaded this young man. He quickly realised that just above the informal, usually hassle-free drug-getting arrangements of 'friends of friends' of a dealer there was a commercial business at work which used fairly aggressive market-protection strategies.

We were cutting out Towling's main dealer, we were cutting out . . . Eastmoor's main dealers and they weren't very happy, and they started coming down quite heavy. . . . I think the worst was . . . I was at college and all these guys surrounded the car I was in and said 'get out the car otherwise we're going to shoot you through the window'. The police turned up . . . everything got sorted.

(Gary, poly drug user)

Similarly two female friends from the sample found themselves followed by the police to a drug dealer's house and arrested, charged and cautioned:

Once on the train two CID told me to get off the train. We recognised them. They'd followed me from Beachtown. We'd been walking round town all day smoking, right off it. They took all my details and gave me a caution. I only had £10 or an eighth's worth of weed on me but I must have led CID right to the weed hut [the dealers]. I haven't been back since. I don't think I'd be too welcome.

(Year 5, critical incident interview)

This same pair had become nightclubbers and ravers and had many tales to tell about door staff and dealers in clubs. Stories about trouble, 'taxing' and the more serious and dangerous end of drug dealing helped draw the line about where relative safety ended and potential trouble began. Thus whilst simply buying drugs from dealers in nightclubs was risky in terms of quality it was relatively safe in terms of not meeting any 'heavy duty' people; but things change radically if you get involved with door staff, club 'territory' or selling for profit. Similarly getting your drugs via the friend of a friend of a dealer was relatively safe in terms of both quality and avoiding police surveillance. However, start to move up the chains and networks either to get better value supplies or to make money for yourself and the drugs–crime connection is made and you become of interest both to the Drugs Squad and more organised criminal dealers.

Finally, a tragic 'dealing' case needs reporting. One of our respondents and her friend were caught trafficking in cocaine and they are both serving lengthy sentences in a South American jail. Whilst we only have information supplied by letters and an interview with one mother it appears that the two girls became 'mules' for a Nigerian man who persuaded them to smuggle cocaine. This was one case where a local story became a global story – where a community tale and a media sensation merged.

In summary, the steep climb in availability and offer rates described in Chapter 4, whilst they help us measure the significant penetration of illicit drugs into the social space of adolescence, fail to capture the routinisation of all this: the frequency of repeated availability and offer situations. Moreover drugs are not 'pushed' at young people as the 'war on drugs' discourse would have it. Most obtain their drugs from friends of friends and have genuine difficulty in perceiving these acquaintances as dealers committing a potentially serious criminal act. Whilst a handful of our cohort became more instrumental dealers and moved into making a financial profit, most low-level 'dealers' in our cohort at most covered the cost of their own drug use. This accommodation, some might say colonisation of drugs 'supplying' within youth culture, is an important feature of the normalisation debate to which we will return.

Trying drugs

Initiation

We have already noted that initiation, or the first time drug trying 'incidence' which drove up our lifetime prevalence rates, takes place throughout adolescence. Cannabis dominates as the first drug ever tried throughout:

> That was pot . . . I think I was about 13 . . . with my sister and my mates. These lads who had it, we got in with them, they'd been smoking it for a while; but it was our first time.
>
> [How did you know what to do?] I didn't, they did it for us, it looked dead complicated to me.
>
> [Had you smoked cigarettes before?] Yes I've been smoking since I was about eleven.
>
> [Was the spliff easy to inhale?] No, it choked me at first.
>
> [Get any effect?] Oh, very easy. I'd only had a couple of pulls and I was sitting there giggling my head off. It was brilliant. Because like when you're at school, and all of your homework and all the teachers moaning and you, you know . . . so the first time, I can remember that night, I felt brilliant.

[Anything bad about it?] No. Only when I came in and my mum and dad looking at my eyes. I was terrified . . . but they didn't know.

(Lisa, drug user)

These early experiences are often reviewed and perhaps redefined with time, as in this next case by a young women who became a serious drug user by 17:

Yes I was drunk at the time and I was in a nightclub. I was only 14. I used to have a Saturday job and we all went out. It was only pot but at the time I thought it was brilliant. And I was drunk and I most probably didn't understand and probably not even smoking it properly. That was the first time, that was pot that was it . . . it was different, it was just a bit more relaxed. I just personally think there's nothing wrong with it. OK, 14 is a bit young, but it's not really a hard drug or anything.

[Did you know what to do?] No. Not really at the time, we were just looking at everybody else . . . because you don't know you just pick up what other people do.

(Zoe)

We noted in Chapter 4 that in mid adolescence amphetamines and LSD were also common initiation drugs:

Speed, sixteen with five friends.

[Where did you get it from?] My friend's boyfriend's mate. I just dabbed it they snorted it.

[How did you know what to do?] Well basically they'd done it before and just said do you want to snort it and I said no, so they said well put it in a cigarette paper and I said oh no and then they said well just dab it then and take it that way. So they gave me the options . . . it tasted completely horrible.

[Did you think it was worth it?] After the very first time no.

[Anything positive?] When it started to come up on me then I felt it was easier for me to talk to people and to go along with people and I felt more relaxed and open.

[Anything negative?] At the end I didn't feel very well. I wasn't hungry, I felt a bit depressed as well even though I'd only taken it the once.

[Any other drugs at the same time?] Just alcohol.

[And the feeling?] Not very easy at first, my mates were actually speeding when I was still bobbing along... they said 'oh it'll work, you'll find out when it works'. I think it was an hour and a half before I'd actually... for it to come up on me.

[How long were you up for?] All night, all morning, it was well into the next day before we actually got any sleep.

[How much had you had?] We bought it in fivers and we split it into £2.50s worth each. Maybe that was it, I'd never had it before, so maybe I'd taken too much for the first time.

(Vicky, regular drug user)

LSD in particular sometimes proved an unpleasant first-time experience. An experienced regular poly drug user at 18, one young woman recalls her initiation:

The first drug I took was LSD. It was horrible... once I came up – all the lads had taken them before – none of the girls had because we all took them together this night – they said you'll go home and you won't want to go in, you'll be that frightened, that paranoid, you won't want to go in. I thought 'Yeah yeah' but then I got outside and I was standing outside my house for two hours, I didn't want to go in. I was supposed to be in at 10 o'clock and I got in at midnight. So I got battered for coming in late. It was horrible. I came in and put on some videos and some music and then it was alright.

(Kate)

Yet although LSD warning stories were common they tended to become more instrumental in later adolescence given that, despite its unpredictability, most users had early positive experiences of trying it:

Me and my friend took LSD when we went to a travelling fair. There was me and my friend and three others, and I think the other people got a bit fed up of us, because we just spent the whole time laughing and messing around, which was a good experience when I was on LSD. Then we went back to the fair the following year, we didn't find it funny at all because we weren't on drugs. That kind of situation, if I was to go back there again I might take LSD again.

[It made it better?] It made it better, yes. And, we went to Stratford with school, to see a play, and we were on LSD and we

were just laughing all the way through that. That was weird . . .
Shakespeare . . . we found Shakespeare extremely funny.

(Elaine)

In later adolescence first time use may well involve ecstasy as the
initiation drug. This, as we have already discussed, is related to new
ventures and values linked to obtaining adult status. One young
woman holidaying with her parents reported her first experience on
ecstasy as follows:

I met them in a bar. Three lads from Stockport and some girls.
And we were just drinking like you do and went into a club and
they were all taking it. They offered me some and I said no at first
and then I was a bit curious so I said yes. And actually I was
amazed at the amount of energy I had . . . it was so different to
how I imagined and a lot better than I thought it would be . . . you
just felt really good about yourself, and confident.

(Joanne)

Asked if her parents guessed she'd been on ecstasy, she replied: 'no, no
they think I'm far too sensible!'

Those who initiated on ecstasy tended to be over 16 and many
accepted that their interest in dance music and the excitement of the
dance club scene led to contemplation which, once in the setting,
produced the trigger: 'I suppose the atmosphere of clubs makes me
want to try . . . it's not really because my friends are doing it, it's
because I want to experiment myself' (Lee, occasional drug user).

Reasons for trying drugs

It is very difficult to write authoritatively about why anyone first tries an
illicit drug. A myriad of factors may be at work. Clearly age, gender,
race, the setting, the actual type of drug and probably the people one is
with, will interact in a complex way with the disposition of the person,
both generally and at the particular time for any individual decision. In
the last chapter we showed how abstainers hold particular attitudes and
beliefs and possibly are distinctive personality types. They will respond
quite differently to the same setting compared with a more adventurous
'curious' person. To further complicate matters reasons for trying or
experimenting with a drug are likely to be different from those moti-
vating repeated use. We analysed the motivational accounts given by our
interviewees as to why they had or hadn't ever tried a drug given almost

all had had such 'trying' opportunities or knew how to create them. *Availability, curiosity* and the presence of *peers* and *friendship networks* who could provide the encouragement, reassurance and know-how were seen as most important. These factors were then mediated by each interviewee's view of themselves and their own *moral* perspective and views of *risk* for health, fitness or vocation, and, in early to mid adolescence in particular, the views or potential responses of their *parents*.

The impact of all these factors will be different for each person and indeed as we saw in the Pathways analysis the weight given to each factor by a young person may well change through time.

Drug-trying interviewees nominated curiosity and friendship patterns and influences as the most important factors involved in initial experimentation and trying a range of drugs. These factors usually combine as explained by a cannabis user who has also tried LSD and amphetamines but was, at 18, becoming more cautious:

> Mainly curiosity. Me and my close friend . . . you hear that people have good times on drugs, so you feel like doing it yourselves.
> [Any other things?] Not really, just the fact that they were around. If there'd been other drugs around at the time [when 15 years] say maybe ecstasy, then I might have done but it wasn't really in our age groups.
>
> (Elaine)

> I suppose that all my friends were. Just wanted to try it. It's all very well saying how bad things are, but until you've tried it you don't really know these things, do you.
>
> (Sandra, poly drug user)

The dominant view of why young people take drugs, portrayed in the media and encapsulated in government policy, relegates curiosity and choice in favour of peer pressure. Yet it is extremely difficult to measure peer pressure. Even if one observed a drug initiation in a peer-group setting it would be problematic, merely using personal accounts, to make a safe assessment. Furthermore young people are encouraged in their wider education to be self-assertive and not be unduly influenced by others and many young people would not wish to be perceived or perceive themselves as being a 'victim' of such pressure. This said, the rejection of peer pressure as a significant factor was almost unanimous amongst our interviewees (only five of the sixty-three interviewees who were asked or answered the specific question about peer pressure felt they had been affected by it).

For the majority, certainly at the age of 18 and looking back, the statements below were typical:

> I've not really been pressured into taking them or anything. I'd say that everytime that I've done something its been my own decision.
>
> (Martin, poly drug user)

> What level of mood I'm in . . . the place I'm in, the environment and the people I'm with.
>
> [What about when you first started taking drugs?] I think the first reason I started was because everybody else was and I thought well I'll just try it.
>
> [Any peer pressure?] No, nobody would pressure me to do it, I just saw everybody else having a good time and good laugh.
>
> (Vicky, poly drug user)

Interestingly however, when we undertook a content analysis of the interviews, we found that several more interviewees described events and recounted episodes where at least one interpretation could be that they had been strongly influenced by their peers:

> When we got into the gang, everyone was doing it in the club, and I was going to say no because of my brother [serious drug problems] but my mate said 'come on we're having them, you have to have them too because you might feel like the odd one out, like the weirdo if you're not doing it'. I'd say one of the reasons why was because everyone else was doing it.
>
> (Helen)

This young woman did appear to come from a fairly dysfunctional family and was receiving counselling. The interviewer's feedback suggested she was fairly vulnerable in a number of ways. Another young woman felt that she had been under pressure at 14.

> When I was in school, I had my first trip, it was with my best friend and her sisters, and I didn't really want to and they were saying 'go on, go on', so I had half . . . and I've never touched trips since.

However at 16 she began a drug-using career which has continued into dance club-related ecstasy use:

Curiosity, friends I suppose and I was 16 when I was going out with my boyfriend and he used to always go to the Big Bar and I never used to drink and they always seemed to be on a different planet, and I always used to wonder, and I used to feel left out I suppose and I wanted to know what kind of wavelength they were on.

[So drugs?] Just to say I'd tried them once really. And just to know for myself if I liked them or I didn't want them.

(Diane)

Questionnaire surveys of young people's drug use appear to be able to quantify their decision-making processes. Indeed it is not difficult to set a closed question asking a sample 'do you think young people try drugs because their friends encourage them?' and conclude that peer pressure is significant. Conversely, ask sample of 18-year-olds who've made up their minds about drugs whether they feel they've been pushed or pressured into their conclusions and they will, on reflection, tend to deny this, thereby apparently rejecting peer pressure. This gets us nowhere. We have a set of phrases in official drugs discourse – peer pressure, peer preference, peer influence – to which we might add peer example and peer support. In the end adolescence is a life phase where peers are central to most decisions and activities and we can have the same unhelpful debate about whether school performance, participation in sport, joining community groups or whatever is related to peer behaviour. And even if we could isolate and quantify the effects of peers we can do little about this. The dominant way of caring for and controlling children and teenagers is to herd them together in schools for most of their waking hours for most weeks of each year and for at least eleven years. Moreover the key thing young people want to do in their free time is to be with their friends.

A myriad of variables can be identified in drug-initiation and drug-trying events. We have shown that availability of drugs, disposable income, curiosity, friends who do drugs, friends who don't do drugs, drugwiser acquaintances who can guide and support novices, being drunk, have a certain outlook on risk taking and rule breaking; parental influences, religious and moral frameworks, the impact of 'drugs stories' may all be found to impact on decisions. However, beyond identifying the complexity and multifacticity of drug-trying events, it is probably impossible to weight different factors in any generalisable way. It is most certainly unsafe to collapse this complexity into monocausal 'soundbites' such as peer pressure.

The cost-benefit assessment

Each drug is different

Before describing the cost-benefit assessment which broadly guides each young person's journey into becoming a user of one or more 'recreational' drugs we need to recall the general consensus which emerged from the surveys about the positive and negative effects of each of the main recreational drugs. In this section we concentrate on cannabis, amphetamines, LSD and ecstasy, these being the most widely used drugs (solvents and magic mushrooms as 'trying only' drugs are not discussed here and poppers are only referred to in the context of dance drug use).

Heroin and crack cocaine are important to our analysis primarily because of their symbolic value. Despite their apparent sophistication about their own drugs of choice, 1990s' adolescents maintain a fairly stereotypical imaging of hard drug users as dangerous, diseased, dishevelled injecting 'junkies' and 'saddos' who commit vast amounts of crime to fund their habit. For most of this age cohort the idea of taking hard drugs and actually injecting a drug is an anathema: a Rubicon they will not cross. If heroin and crack are at one end of the spectrum cannabis is at the other. Cannabis is regarded, even by many abstainers, as a relatively safe drug and certainly no more dangerous than alcohol and tobacco. Its predictability, steady quality and price and 'sociability' are celebrated along with its ability to induce relaxation, reduce stress and mediate sleep patterns.

The other three have a more ambivalent status. Few who are drug-wise doubt the potential positive enjoyment of LSD, amphetamines and ecstasy but there are risks with each and the unpredictability of any particular dose causes many potential triers or users to reflect carefully as they make their cost-benefit assessment.

The key point is that those moving into regular drug use judge each drug or combination on its merits. They begin with the premise that each drug is different. They see themselves as far more sophisticated about this than their elders, be they parents or politicians, who, they conclude, tend to see drugs as generically bad and dangerous.

The assessment formula

As we have shown in Chapter 5, trying drugs, usually for free via a friend, is not the same as using drugs regularly. Regular use is an act of consumption which involves, directly or indirectly, the *purchase* of the chosen drugs, which in turn involves a decision about expending limited disposable income. The fact that these transactions are *illegal* and that there is a risk attached to being caught with drugs at school, college, work or through routine policing are also relevant. Each drug also carries a potential health risk. The exact nature of this risk is diffuse and hard to quantify but divides into several components. There is an *immediate* risk of a bad experience, incident or accident. The longer term *health impact* of a particular drug or combination may be relevant but again hard to quantify. Possible *dependency* and addiction is another potential concern. Then there are the *side* or *after effects* of drug-using episodes. For some, these unwanted effects are significant 'risks' but for many experienced users they are seen as part and parcel of knowing and understanding a drug. So what would be regarded as a dreadful risk for an abstainer would be seen as the accepted consequences of 'getting out of it' by an amphetamine user.

Finally we need to place *leisure and pleasure* in the formula. Drugs are used because they give enjoyment. Young drug users who spend their disposable income on alcohol, cannabis or ecstasy are, in their own minds, making rational decisions about hedonistic consumption. Essentially they are using a *cost-benefit equation*. Whilst it would be unwise to suggest that every young drug user in the study utilised this formula comprehensively and explicitly, almost all our interviewees eluded to most components of the formula in describing their motivational accounts and decision making journeys into recreational drug use.

Before illustrating each component of the cost-benefit equation we should remember to place all this in context since, by definition, we are only capturing a brief period, mainly around 16 –18, in this 'journeys' analysis. Given that we know that the 'onset' of drug use spans adolescence and continues into young adulthood then the nature and sophistication of decision making will be mediated by age, intellect and maturity whereby the quality of decisions at age 14 is likely to be very different from those taken at age 19. Undertaking high risk behaviour with little insight into the possible consequences is sometimes referred to as adolescents' perceiving themselves as *invulnerable* (Plant and Plant, 1992). One young woman although quite unaware of the terminology had no doubt about its impact:

> You kind of go through a phase when you're 14–15 when you do a lot of things like that [take trips at school] and then when you get older you realise that, when you're at that age you think that nothing can happen to you, whereas when you get older you

realise that it is actually dangerous. I don't think pot is dangerous. I'll do that again.

(Elaine)

Other interviewees recognised they had failed to understand the significance of early drug trying but put a quite different spin on their conclusions:

The money. Your sleeping patterns. You get in with some bad people.

[Money?] I used to go out four nights a week, and I had a part-time job and all my wages and more, I ended up owing nearly £400.

[Did you pay it off?] Yes. I stayed in for four months.

[And sleeping patterns?] I used to have speed all the time, so I never used to sleep and when I started getting to sleep it was 6 o'clock in the morning . . . and I was getting up for school.

[Bad people?] One of my mates is only 17 and he's been involved in an armed robbery . . . but I've never been in trouble with the police.

[Do you see your drug use as normal, OK or unusual, a problem?] It was a problem I suppose . . . I've decided not to make it a problem now. I used to sit there and think . . . I wished I wasn't curious. If I hadn't had the first one . . . or if I hadn't done them till I was 18 it would have been different . . . like I used to do a lot of sport at school, now I don't do anything. . . . I passed everything then I failed my medical to get into the army because I'd been doing the stuff I was doing at school.

(Roy)

For this respondent the costs to his finances, his health, his energy and his career prospects had all proved far greater than he, as a 14-year-old, had been able to calculate. With these provisos we can now describe the various facets of the cost-benefit assessment.

Relaxation, enjoyment and a 'buzz'

In Chapter 4 we summarised the positive and negative effects our survey respondents attached to each widely used drug. We noted that those who had used a particular drug listed far more positives than negatives. Cannabis users and poly drug users who include cannabis in their repertoire speak confidently about its enjoyment value: 'I just like the effect, it relaxes me. And you can buzz off it sometimes if you're stoned, just buzz off the littlest things' (Lucy, cannabis user).

It's sort of, when you go out and try and enjoy yourself and it's a sort of way of bringing on the enjoyment I suppose. It helps you relax. It's just something to do. It's sort of basically getting a bit of a buzz really.

(Neil, cannabis user)

[Cannabis?] It just relaxes me. I'm able to get into things a bit better . . . It gets a lot of pressures out of you, cannabis just makes me feel a bit easier.

(Jason, poly drug user)

Poly drug users note the distinctive role of cannabis in their chosen drugs repertoire. One young female single parent, noted:

When it's pot, it's just to unwind, when I'm with the baby all day and night in the week, if you ever get a free night it's to unwind really, relax, have a change.
[What about speed?] That's whenever I go out, you know with the baby I'm tired all the time. When I start getting ready to go out of a Saturday night, so it makes us a bit energetic.

(Lisa, poly drug user)

Another poly drug user compared ecstasy with her more regular diet of alcohol and cannabis:

Favourite . . . E, even though I don't take it anymore.
[Why E?] Because you just feel so different, it's just, I can't explain, it's just such a wonderful feeling. You see everything in a different light, everyone seems so nice, and everyone's dead friendly. When everybody else is having it as well, you can do what you want and no one thinks you're a dick.
[What effects do you particularly like about it?] The good feeling. The feeling that you can go on all night.
[Where do you prefer to have it?] At a club, an all-night club.

Having realised that ecstasy brought on her asthma attacks this young woman had reluctantly removed it from her repertoire. Asked about her favourite combinations she noted:

Usually just have alcohol and weed and cigs as well. If I'm on a whizz as well I smoke weed but not usually if I'm on E.
[Your favourite combination?] Yes, alcohol and weed.
[Order?] Usually have weed first then go out for a drink.
[The aims?] To try and get happy and relaxed.
[Anything else?] No that's about it.

(Kate, poly drug user)

Risks and dangers

Family responses

Parental condemnation of their children's drug use appeared to be total at the beginning of the 1990s. Indeed the development of widespread recreational drug use in adolescence for the first time produced genuine concern amongst most adults. In early adolescence our samples were almost unanimously of the view that if their parents found out they were taking drugs then 'mega' trouble would follow. This situation still held for the majority of interviewees even at 18:

I know my dad would go absolutely mental 'cos he works with loads of people that have gone over the boundary and took too many drugs. He works as a counsellor. My mum would go mad as well.

(Sandra, drug user)

[Do your parents know you take drugs?] No, oh God no. Terrible. They'd go absolutely mad, they really would. I don't think they'd throw me out or anything, but I think it would put something between us.

(Suzanne)

However near the end of the study there were signs that this clash of minds was not inevitable. A third of drug-taking interviewees confirmed that one or both parents knew something about their drug use. Cannabis is perceived by both parties as 'the least worst' drug both for parents to hear about and children to admit to:

Problems? No not really, my mum asked me not so long ago if I had ever taken cannabis, I said yes, that was really hard on her but I told her I don't take it regularly.

(Neil, drug trier, cannabis user)

One interviewee arrested via a routine police stop was charged with possession of cannabis for which, after admitting the offence, he was given a police caution. His parents, although very shocked: 'were sound about it. It's just that if I get caught again the last one will be brought up. It worries me a bit but not to a great extent. . . . They don't know about anything else' (Martin).

What this young man's parents didn't know is that their son's favourite drugs combination, of ecstasy and amphetamine, makes up a regular weekly clubbing diet. Poly drug users were typically economical with the truth, feeling the 'cannabis card' was the only one to play at home:

I'd be a dead man . . . my mum would kill me and my dad, because he's taken it he'd chat with me and talk about it. He's already said he wouldn't mind me smoking gange. He said 'if you're going to do it, just tell me. I'll probably join you on a session', but he said 'if you ever got into any heavy stuff, I'd kill you'.

(Gary, poly drug user)

Few respondents felt their parents could cope with anything more than cannabis admissions:

Yes mum knows about cannabis.
[Was she shocked about it?] She was when she found out but I gave her a leaflet. . . . I don't think they'd appreciate me doing ecstasy but with cannabis they accept it as a social thing.

(Andy, poly drug user)

Parental 'ignorance' is seen as the main reason for potential disagreement and trouble. So even upon entering young adulthood when the authority element in the parent–child relationship declines interviewees felt it was not usually worth standing their grown-up ground and pointing out that their drug use is recreational and nothing to worry about. Parents simply think the worst:

. . . my dad. He's just completely against it.
[Because its illegal?] Yes. Well and because he doesn't like drugs.
[Are the arguments about drugs regular?] Yes. But I just say its my life. He knows I smoke the weed, I've told him so there's nothing he can do about it . . .
[Can he differentiate between different types of drugs?] No. He puts them all together. He thinks, like, when I said I smoke the

weed dad would say I was a druggie. He thinks you have to inject it into your arm or something, he doesn't know the facts . . . you can't get through to him.

(Lucy, cannabis user)

Concern for parental feelings via 'white lies' was not unusual but we should remember the mum whose daughter is in an overseas prison and the parents of those teenagers whose delinquent and drug careers overlap and bring chaos to family life. Adolescent behaviour can also be beyond the pale and thus extremely painful and difficult for parents:

At first they didn't have a clue. They knew I smoked weed and tolerated it, as long as it was in my bedroom. They would just leave me be. They couldn't stop me. Then I came back one New Year's Eve and they clicked. My parents do my head in now because one, they blame everything on drugs if we argue about anything, and two, they know I don't do weed but they don't believe I've stopped taking other stuff. I used to rob lots of money, £200 or more. That's why there's locks on all the upstairs doors. If you went upstairs you'd see all the locks. I argued with them, broke windows, got chucked out. I left school, blew a thousand pounds in three weeks, lived with my mate. In the end they just tolerated it, in the end. They had no choice. I smoked spliffs all day. I got kicked out, left school. I had a thousand pounds in a bank savings account and I blew it. I moved in with my mate 'cos her parents went away. Dad phoned me every day to ask me to come home. I came home when her parents came back.

(joint interview Year 5, female poly drugs users)

Friends and partners

The risk of causing trouble and upset in the family home extends, naturally, to equally significant others' namely friends and partners. Traditionally, self-selecting friends with similar outlooks, interests and attitudes has mediated tensions caused by difference which becomes dissonance. Outgoing, smoking and drinking socialisers befriend fellow-revellers and eschew abstainers. Equally such risk takers would not be chosen companions for more cautious, rule-keeping adolescents. Whilst this self-selection continues to operate it is clearly no longer able to prevent disagreements surfacing. We saw how the impact of differential attitudes to drug use distinguished abstainers from drug users and those in transition in the pathways analysis. Yet once we explore relationships within drug user networks we find similar discord. This is because through the cost-benefit assessment distinctive personal limits are defined. One young woman who had a frightening experience with ecstasy has 'never touched it since'; yet her friends continue to use dance drugs:

> My friend said 'you should have half and go to the cinema' to get back your confidence' [with ecstasy] but I just don't want to get . . . but everybody . . . I'm abnormal to my friends, they used to have them in school . . . to them, I'm abnormal for not ever wanting to do it again.
>
> (Diane)

Similarly an amphetamine-using respondent felt caught up in club-drug culture expectations:

> I was in the toilet with my best friend and she took drugs and she was a lot older headed than me and she brought another girl and there were four of us all together and she said her friend had bought two Es . . . a half each. 'No I don't take them' I said and Tara started going off her head . . . 'what do you think you're doing, she just bought you one, you should take it', so I said 'well I don't want to take it' so we ended up having a fight about it, a proper fight, and ended up getting thrown out of the club because I wouldn't take it. And I said never, not one would ever touch my lips. I'd take a whizz but not an E because I've heard all the . . . you have your first one and you're dead.
>
> (Suzanne)

Such experiences can lead to reassessment about friendship patterns and support the importance of peer preferences:

> I was involved as well, we took an E, or I think it was and they didn't know what it was or anything, it was awful, they were just off their heads . . . it really scares me. Yes and then they took another one and mixed two types. They didn't know if it was off or anything, they were really stupid, they were drunk as well at the time, so that made it worse and it was just really scary. I hadn't seen them like that before . . . I think I've grown away from them

since that, after that incident. Me and my other friend have just
stayed away.

(Natalie, reducing drug user)

As with drinking together so taking drugs together can set friends
against each other:

I've had arguments with my friends occasionally.
[What are the arguments about?] It's me as well as my friends,
but I've got a friend in particular who tends to get quite aggressive
sometimes when she's taking drugs and she'll tend to snarl and
snap at you a lot, so it tends to cause arguments between us. And
myself, I tend to be more aggressive with her back, so it does cause
problems that way.

(Sandra, drug user).

Romantic relationships were regularly discussed in the context of
drug use. Most often it would be along traditional gender lines
whereby there were far more boyfriends under scrutiny for excessive
drug use and a lecture the day after:

He didn't actually tell me he took cocaine, I heard it from his
brother and the first time he had it he got it free and then the
second time he got it free as well because it was a close friend of
his who had it. I just thought if he was going to get it free all the
time he'd keep taking it. To me cocaine is like a very very hard
drug, whereas LSD doesn't seem that bad.

(Elaine, drug user)

My boyfriend, when he was smoking skunk, he gets extremely
paranoid off it – I haven't had any of that particular type and he
thought I was carrying on with one of his friends, so it got out of
hand and there was a fight, and it was all totally innocent. It was
just his imagination running away with him.

(Karen, poly drug user)

Occasionally all roles are reversed as the female user is required to
save the male abstainer from hedonism:

My boyfriend was on about taking a trip. He's a bit snobby, so
it was dead upsetting. He's always been dead law abiding and
strict, and someone who keeps me on the straight and narrow.

And he was on about taking them as well so it was a bit worrying.

(Sandra, poly drug user)

In summary, because drugs are illegal and because they produce 'attitude' from almost everybody, the potential drug user has to consider the import of their usage on significant others. Whilst parental wrath and indeed upset and pain is usually a major consideration during adolescence this mutates with the move into young adulthood so that protecting parents from unnecessary worry apparently justifies either continued denial or being very 'economical with the truth'. Friendships can also be disturbed or even fractured because disagreements emerge about the acceptability of both drugs taken and styles of use. Romantic relationships in particular seemed to produce disagreements and the need for compromise or change in respect of drugs. All this said, the fact that there is so much debate amongst young people about each other's drugs views is also indicative of the significance of penetration of 'recreational' drug use into mainstream youth culture.

Health risks and bad experiences

Weighing up the chances of frightening experiences and/or damaging one's physical or psychological health is the central plank – the spinal column – of the cost-benefit assessment. Whether one is an abstainer, trier or regular user, reaching conclusions about this aspect of risk, certainly by late adolescence, appears to be universal. However, longer term health risks are rarely mentioned spontaneously, although when prompted some regular drug users will acknowledge that they have a general worry about the longer term effects of their habits:

I do worry about it in the future I think, it's not a worry so's I wouldn't do it, I just worry about, like if I was pregnant or something and I didn't know, and I'd taken something, that kind of thing. My friend, she's a year older than me, and she drank and she had a trip, and she didn't know (that she was pregnant), but I always wonder how John is going to . . . because he's fine now, but maybe when he goes to school . . . because they don't really know do they.

(Diane, poly drug user)

The absence of spontaneous mention of distant 'morbidity' in normally flowing accounts is compatible with the notion of adolescent invulnerability. Yet we must juxtapose this with the acceptance of vulnerability in spontaneous, animated discussion about bad experiences and *immediate* health risks which, usually in the form of 'drugs stories', dominate the cost-benefit discourse of our young subjects.

This said we also need to distinguish between bad experiences and effects on health which for abstainers and cautious triers would be defined as negative outcomes and real risk, but which for regular users with particular levels of risk tolerance are basically to be endured as part-and-parcel of using a particular drug. Regular poly users often accepted the occasional 'whitey' from too much cannabis, the possibility of flashbacks after LSD or insomnia after amphetamines:

> Because when you take speed, if you take too much, you can't go to sleep, and when you've had pot, I take it to sit down and relax and I know I'm going to have a good night's sleep, but with speed I'm tossing and turning all night and getting up and going to the toilet and coming down stairs. I can't get settled when I've had speed, even though you've been dancing all night.
>
> (Lisa)

Ecstasy and poly drug users in dance clubs had their own package of after effects which many perceived as an acceptable, expected price:

> Pains in the legs the next morning from dancing.
>
> [Anything else?] From smoking weed I get really bad munchies and I feel really guilty for eating all this chocolate.
>
> [Any other disadvantages?] No. I've got a sore jaw the next morning, and I've got ulcers off where I've been chewing gum.
>
> [Does your drug use effect any other part of your life?] The next day I can't really seem to concentrate or anything, I can't do anything too demanding, I'm just tired. It's the same as if you've got a hangover though. It's not like – I've got a friend, she used to take quite a lot – I go out every one or two months, have half or three-quarters, and she used to give it a week to recover and then she used to really look a mess and her skin went horrible.
>
> (Diane)

> [Does it affect any other aspects of your life?] Yes.
>
> [In what way?] Smoking it at college I don't want to do any work, so college work goes down. If I'm taking whizz or some-

thing at a weekend it takes me a week to come down properly, so I can't be arsed to do anything during the week.

(Kate)

Sometimes diagnosing the cause of minor ailments is difficult in that drug use may or may not be relevant:

I suffered from a lot of headaches at one time. I went to see a doctor about my headaches, but I told my mum I was suffering from headaches, and she said 'well you need to go to the doctors, I'll take you', and I said 'no, I'll go on my own'.

[Did you tell him/her about drug use?] Yes. I told her I'd occasionally taken speed.

[What did she say?] Well she obviously told me it was bad for me and should try and knock it on the head. She said it could be [to do with speed], she couldn't exactly be sure of it, but she asked me how often I'd taken it, and I told her it was about once a week, but she didn't actually think it was enough to actually cause headaches unless I was taking it in huge amounts.

[How was she with you?] She was really just down to earth, she wasn't at all funny with me or anything.

[Did you actually believe it might be related to speed?] Yes, I did actually.

[Did you do anything about it, or carry on taking it?] I personally thought it was because of the speed I was suffering the headaches, so I told my doctor and I told my boyfriend about it, so he went berserk, and he told me he wasn't going to let me take it anymore, and I should calm myself down. But I still suffer from them anyway. I went for an eye test and all that kind of thing to see if it was that, but it wasn't and then I just gradually started taking it again.

(Louise)

Other illnesses were clearly drug related:

We went to the doctors because I got complications, I went for a scan, I had kidney problems, and he just said 'have you been on drugs' I said 'no'. He goes 'I know you're lying to me', I said 'how do you know, you're not me'. He goes 'well I'm your doctor, I've known you since you were a baby', so I go 'well OK then, if you think I've been taking drugs, what do you think I'm on?'. He goes 'the symptoms you've got and your health problems', he said 'there's loads of drugs inside you . . . anyone could tell that you've been taking drugs, you want to lay off it, or your kidneys . . . going to be . . . damaged'. I said 'so?', I said 'it's my life I'll do what I want'. He goes 'fine, Helen, I'm your doctor, I'm here to advise you on things' but I wasn't interested, and then he just come to our's one night . . . and my dad goes 'we know about the problem'. He just left a few leaflets and that and said 'if you want to do what you want to do in the future you've got to stop it now', I just told him to mind his own business, 'you're not my father are you, you're just a doctor, nothing to do with me'. So he just walked away, but now I get on fine, and keep going to him and getting tablets.

[Have you told him now?] Yes, he knows, he's one of the people who helped me through the drug things as well, he helped me through, he just said 'I'm glad you got your head together'.

(Helen)

This young woman would perhaps be described on her family doctor's records as anxious, depressed and perhaps volatile by way of a warning to colleagues who might have to treat her. This reminds us that young people take drugs for different reasons and that vulnerable and damaged adolescents are probably even more likely to seek solace in drugs and in turn be more susceptible to 'misusing' them. Another respondent looking back on a very troubled adolescence was beginning to realise her own low self-esteem could not be permanently overcome chemically:

Because . . . it's weird when I take drugs I don't stop eating, and I can go to sleep straight away. Everyone else I know they won't eat for another two days, and they won't go to sleep. I go straight to sleep and I'll have pudding, chips and gravy on the way home. I don't know what's wrong with me. So I thought what's the point, I'm just going to get even fatter. I think the only reason why I took a bit of whizz was because I was putting on weight, and I thought 'I'll take some of this, and I'll lose some weight'. But I didn't get nowhere . . . I have put on a lot of weight since last year.

[Is that since you stopped the whizz?] No, it's more boredom really. I just can't remember what I used to do. I used to go to the army cadets on a Thursday and a Tuesday, and then I stopped all that.

(Suzanne, poly drug user)

One of the key reasons for defining and assessing risks associated with drug use is to avoid bad experiences, sudden illness or loss of control as a direct consequence of drug use. Drug stories are thus important to cautious users and abstainers because they can be used to affirm or reaffirm their declaration not to take any, or particular, drugs:

> LSD? I told you about my friend [bad trip]. I'm scared to take it. I've always been scared to take it but that backed up my idea about being scared because my friend kept getting flashbacks and had to go for drugs counselling.
>
> (John, cannabis user)

> My mate's boyfriend, he got a tablet when he went out to a club, but it was a dodgy one. One of his mates when they were coming home, they were driving, they had to keep stopping the car, he was throwing up everywhere. His other mate couldn't hear nothing, and he just felt like shit all night, he hadn't slept all night, and in the morning he went to the doctors and he was dehydrated and everything. And he said 'if you'd left it another day and not really drank enough', he said 'you would have been dead'. So that was a scare, and he hasn't been out for a few weeks.
>
> [Has he had another tablet?] No, that was the last time. He has trips now.
>
> (Lisa)

> I know someone who was at a club with all his friends and he took drugs, and he was dancing, and he didn't have anything, no water or anything to drink, and he had a bit of fit on the floor and his mates started to panic, and just one of his mates sorted him out, rang the ambulance, and he was taken off and sorted out.
>
> [Did you know that you're recommended to drink water?] Well I knew that it's not a good idea just to dance all night and dehydrate, he should have drank water.
>
> (Ian, drug user)

Having experimented with cannabis, LSD and amphetamines a male, who now uses only cannabis, discussed how he felt about being part of a group of friends with a more extensive drugs repertoire. Quite incidentally, he showed how he'd reached his own limits through recognising the health risks attached to two of these drugs:

I'm not really bothered I suppose, as long as the only drugs they have is cannabis, but LSD and speed, I wouldn't want them to have that all the time, because with speed, as you know, you can lose a lot of weight with it, and it can do your bones in as well, and with LSD it just sends you off to another planet if you keep on having that every day.

[If they used LSD and speed regularly, what would you do?] I'd try and stop them, because it's not good for you at all. If you have them about once every fortnight it's not so bad.

[How often do they use speed and cannabis?] About once a fortnight at most.

(Jason)

For some users the bad experience involves abandoning a particular drug either permanently or at least for a while. One dance drug night-clubber modified her views on drinking and taking ecstasy after one serious incident:

I felt really bad, I stopped dancing, actually sat down and just took myself home. I was sweating cobs as well, I was really, really sweating. I think I did the sensible thing by just calming myself down, sitting down and going home. Because if I would have stayed there . . . well . . . God knows.

[Not what you wanted?] . . . was expecting, just to be a little bit more lively, just to have a bit of a dance and that, because when you've had a few drinks you get tired don't you, when you're really drunk.

[How much did you spend?] £25 on alcohol. The tablets were £10 each. We actually got them cheap as well, they were saying 'because there's a group of you we'll give you these for so much. . . . I felt embarrassed afterwards, I didn't feel as safe as normal, like I thought I was going to faint . . . I was sick the next day . . . the day after I just didn't feel like nothing to eat at all.

(Natalie, poly drug user)

Another poly drug user related her own scary moment merely as a cautionary tale – just one of those things that happen occasionally. She continued to use amphetamines but took greater care with combination use:

It was while I was actually taking the drug. I'd taken speed. I'd taken a bit too much for my body to cope with I suppose, and I felt sick and I started actually being sick and shivering and cold, and then I blacked out.

[How much had you had?] Quite a lot, and I'd been drinking as well, so I think it was a combination of the two.

(Vicky, drug user)

Through observing these sorts of drink–drug mishaps other dance drug users regard them as serious enough to repackage a weekend repertoire. One respondent who had used all the main recreational drugs avoided getting drunk at nightclubs. She'd start her Saturday night with a spliff of cannabis before moving onto her preferred clubbing combinations:

Ecstasy and Rush [poppers] – just for that moment, I wouldn't want it all night. Not all the time, maybe every twenty minutes.

[What order?] Before, usually in the car, because I have to take it [ecstasy] dead early for me to come up because it takes ages. If I take it when I get in there I come up when everyone's going home. Take Rush in there and maybe one half of lager. I've never been drunk on a tablet, I've seen what other people are like, I like to know what I'm doing.

[Anything else? Cannabis at all?] Yes about four o'clock in the morning.

(Diane)

In summary it is the immediate health risks and the chance of having bad experiences particularly with amphetamines, LSD and ecstasy, perhaps combined with alcohol, which dominate the risk concerns of young drug triers and users. Yet the consensus we find at the two ends of the spectrum about cannabis on the one hand and heroin and cocaine on the other is harder to identify with these middle-range drugs. What is an acceptable bad experience for one is a bridge too far for another and the cost-benefit equation cannot fully explain these subjective understandings and thresholds. Significantly whilst pharmacologists and addiction experts (e.g. Saunders, 1997) are debating the long term effects of regular use of drugs like ecstasy our respondents rarely made spontaneous reference to them.

Conclusion

In attempting to describe and analyse drug decision making journeys we have identified a set of repeated elements which are found in the motivational accounts of our interviewees and respondents. In this chapter we have tried to illustrate how clusters of young people journey down particular drugs pathways as they gain experience, take on new information, learn more about themselves and the personal effects of particular drugs. We are also illustrating why so many drug taking opportunities are *rejected*, why cannabis-only users won't even try another drug, why for some LSD is a taboo drug whilst ecstasy is acceptable and so on.

The cost-benefit equation is a conceptual tool, a dynamic framework to help us understand these journeys. It should not become a mechanical explanation nor should it be used to filter out contradictions. Our young subjects are not immune from exaggerations or distortion nor can they always even adequately define their own relationship with drugs. We have identified some quite damaged and vulnerable young subjects, others with delinquent tendencies and others again who have, by normal standards, excessive appetites for psychoactive highs.

The cost-benefit equation, for instance, *cannot* fully explain whether or not this latter group will continue to journey down poly drugs careers which could end up in dependency and disorder. It does not pretend to include theories of addiction in that growing dependency is often invisible to the user. Whilst the interviewer may have identified signs of psychological dependency, this young woman made no such connection:

> Every time I go out and I don't have it, I think 'oh I'm dying for one ... ' but I can go out and not have anything, but I would prefer to.
>
> [What are you getting out of it?] A good night. I just feel like having that feeling. That's it really.
>
> [Do you crave it?] When I go out, in Beachtown not so much, but if we went to town and I was seeing everybody else. I wouldn't sit here [now] and go 'oh my God I need a tablet', but if you hear the music or something that reminds me of it, I think 'ooh I just fancy one of them'.
>
> (Diane)

In this chapter we have built on the pathways analysis by offering an appreciative perspective of the actual experiential journeys our drug triers and users took during their adolescence, based on the in-depth interviews conducted when the samples were becoming 18. We have hopefully brought to life the issues of drugs availability and the key role friendship and acquaintance networks play in obtaining drugs. The vast majority of our drug users get their drugs via 'friends of friends' or 'friends of dealers'. Aside from the nightclubbers in the sample, direct contact with professional drug dealers is a rare event and sometimes an unhappy one. The dealer–user distinction is both extremely hard to make within this world of recreational drug use yet suddenly abundantly clear when 'real' dealers appear.

In offering oral histories of their drugs initiation and early trying experiences, interviewees emphasised personal curiosity and the support, sometimes encouragement, occasionally 'pressure', of friend-ship networks. Most first-time experiments were with cannabis and were benign. LSD and amphetamines and, in late adolescence, ecstasy were occasionally more problematic and often became significant events captured in a 'drugs story'. Becoming a drug user involves a greater commitment and a more complicated self-assessment. The elements of this assessment were so often repeated in each inter-viewee's accounts that they can be brought together within the cost-benefit equation. This equation assumes that most young people are *drugwise* and that they differentiate between the range of drugs readily available on the youth market in terms of their effects, both positive and negative.

Our young drug triers in the early 1990s nearly all rejected heroin and cocaine out of hand as drugs with dreadful reputations because of their addictive potential and the dangers lurking in the subterranean worlds in which they are dealt and used. 'Hard drugs' currently have no place in the normalisation thesis we have been assessing. Cannabis on the other hand is perceived as a fairly safe drug. The middle three – amphetamines, LSD and ecstasy – are more equivocally defined and when we explore attitudes to and the acceptability of these drugs we find the cost-benefit equation in full flow.

The regular consumption of one or more of the available drugs usually involves a purchasing decision. However for the 'supplier' this transaction is illegal as is possessing each drug. This risk has to be assessed in terms of stigma and censure by parents, partners, friends, teachers and the criminal justice system. Personal relationships and career opportunities might be damaged. The immediate health risks, including scary moments and bad experiences, must also be gauged for each drug or combination. Longer-term health risks are rarely assessed probably because of the lack of available information and lack of agreement amongst the 'experts'.

All these risks and possible costs are compared with the enjoyment that can be obtained from using a particular drug. Here drugs 'culture' offers added value in that being with friends and partners whilst using drugs is usually an important, enjoyable social event. It is part of 'time out' from the grind of most days. But the drug users segment because they reach different cost-benefit conclusions. For many, primarily cannabis users, the 'brilliant' weekends described by the nightclub poly drug users are obtained at far too high a risk.

The cost-benefit assessment is a useful conceptual tool in helping to understand the key elements in each young person's decision-making journey but, unlike the pathways analysis, it cannot explain or predict outcomes. It is not a theory nor should be seen as an always explicit, fully utilised equation to be reduced to a drug user's handbook of rational consumption, for whilst rational decision making usually guides, it may not dominate. Thus, we have identified how a minority of quite damaged and vulnerable young subjects have 'misused' drugs to their cost and how others with delinquent tendencies have got involved in situations which can hardly be described as 'recreational'. This journeys analysis cannot predict how individuals will turn out since it makes no attempt to assess individual propensity to physical or psychological dependency on drugs. Furthermore, numerous other factors would be needed for theory development. On the other hand the articulate and animated debates we have captured demonstrate how deeply entrenched recreational drug use has become in contemporary British youth culture and how to journey through adolescence in 'modern' times makes almost all young people drugwise.

7 Towards the normalisation of recreational drug use

As the 1990s draw to a close the headline figures from the North West Longitudinal Study seem increasingly unremarkable. Snapshot surveys are routinely returning similar drug offer or lifetime drug trying rates. As important as these prevalence surveys have been they have told us little about how and why young Britons have become, in less than a decade, such determined consumers of 'recreational' drugs to the point that we can begin to talk about the normalisation of *this* type of drug use.

Blessed with a well-resourced, longitudinal investigation which has been able to explore drug use in the context of growing up in 'modern' times, by utilising a whole range of methods, we have purposefully concentrated on these explanatory questions. In this final chapter we turn to the implications of the conclusions reached in the earlier chapters. We begin by drawing together the normalisation thesis. Thus we also offer an answer to the question 'to what extent has mainstream youth culture assimilated and legitimated recreational drug use?' Once we move to this more macro, abstract approach we must in turn situate any theorising about drug use in the wider context of the social change which has transformed young people's experiences of growing up with 'late modernity' (Giddens, 1991). It is not the nature of adolescence which has changed but the nature of the experience of growing up. Rapid social changes in so many facets of everyday life have conspired to make growing up today 'feel' far less secure and more uncertain for far longer. In the first chapter we documented these changes in education and training, the youth labour market and work patterns, housing and living arrangements, marriage and parenting decisions and the nature of leisure, which must be increasingly purchased. To grow up today is to grow up in a risk society (Furlong and Cartmel, 1997).

The unprecedented increase in recreational drug use is deeply embedded in these other social processes since such drug use is both about risk taking but also about using 'time out' to self-medicate the impact of the stresses and strains of both success and failure in 'modern' times.

In the final part of this chapter we challenge the current 'war on drugs' discourse developed by consecutive Conservative governments but accepted and maintained by Labour. This whole strategy is based on so many misconceptions and misunderstandings about young people and drugs that it will, in the end, have to be reviewed. By its very nature the process of normalisation demands regulation and *management*. However, the political moment has not yet been reached when the State will accept responsibility for this.

The normalisation of recreational drug use

Although using the term 'recreational' is not without its difficulties, we must begin by emphasising that the normalisation thesis we have developed refers only to the use of certain drugs, primarily cannabis but also nitrites, amphetamines and equivocally LSD and ecstasy. Heroin and cocaine are not included in the thesis. Similarly chaotic combination drug use and dependent 'daily' drug use form no part of our conceptualisation. This is because abstainers, cautious drug users and indeed many of our regular young drug users do not accept or accommodate such approaches to drug taking any more than social drinkers regard violent drunken outbursts or drinking to unconsciousness as an acceptable way to use alcohol. The minority of young people who use 'hard' drugs the hard way are not regarded as recreational drug users by most of their peers.

The concept of normalisation has been used in many contexts but essentially it is concerned with how a 'deviant', often subcultural, population or their deviant behaviour is able to be accommodated into a larger grouping or society. For example, the partial assimilation of people with learning difficulties, previously segregated and 'warehoused', into mainstream communities has often been explained as a process of normalisation (Wolfensberger, 1972).

Normalisation in the context of recreational drug use cannot be reduced to the intuitive phrase 'it's normal for young people to take drugs'; that is both to oversimplify and overstate the case. We are concerned only with the spread of deviant activity and associated attitudes from the margins *towards* the centre of youth culture where it joins many other accommodated 'deviant' activities such as excessive drinking, casual sexual encounters and daily cigarette smoking.

Although tobacco use is clearly normalised and most young people have tried a cigarette only a minority are regular smokers and even then their behaviour is only acceptable to their peers in certain settings. So normalisation need not be concerned with absolutes; we are not even considering the possibility that most young Britons will become illicit drug *users*. It is quite extraordinary enough that we have so quickly reached a situation where the majority will have tried an illicit drug by the end of their teens and that in many parts of the UK up to a quarter may be regular recreational drug users.

The key features of our normalisation thesis are as follows:

Drugs availability

We noted in Chapter 4 the incremental rise in drug offer situations throughout adolescence, so that by the age of 15 a majority of our respondents had been in situations where drugs were available to try or buy and by 18 almost all had been in such situations. In the 'journeys' chapter we showed how behind these figures lie far more potent processes in that drugs are routinely available in school, college, pub and club. Without this ready availability the process of normalisation could not have begun. The commodification of drugs has developed on the back of global processes and it is quite clear that supply cannot be stemmed in free trade, market economies where deregulation, international transport and trade agreements and reductions in frontier controls facilitate drug trafficking as much as legitimate trade (Stares, 1996). Ironically the rise in drugs seizures, often reported as 'success' in the 'war on drugs' discourse, is in fact an indicator of the enormous scale of the movement of undetected illicit drugs.

Drug trying

Although different self-report research techniques produce different rates of drug trying, each approach has plotted sustained upturns during the 1990s. At the beginning of the decade we were finding that one or two in ten young people, by the age of 18, had ever tried a drug. Prevalence has climbed with each adolescent cohort so that from five to six in ten young Britons are now disclosing drug trying by this age. The trend has been quite clear.

The normative nature of drug trying has been further demonstrated by the closure of gender and social class differences. Traditionally far more young men than women would experiment with drugs. During the 1990s this gender difference has closed rapidly and many studies, like our own, actually record no significant differences by sex. In the same way being 'middle class' no longer predicts school-aged abstinence and we are now finding that the offspring of 'professional and managerial' parents often have the highest rates of drug trying followed by young people from the lowest socio-economic backgrounds. Given that being black or Asian does not predict higher than average rates of adolescent drug use the withering of traditional sociological predictor variables is, in political terms, the most challenging aspect of normalisation. If well-behaved, middle class, sixth form pupils are trying drugs and higher education students have voracious drugs appetites (Webb *et al.*, 1996) how can drug trying or use be fundamentally linked to academic failure, delinquency and low self-esteem and thus pathologised. We must also note that drug trying is beginning younger and initiation routinely extends into young adulthood (McKeganey, 1997).

Drug use

We have shown how adolescent decision making journeys have led around a quarter of our samples down the regular drug user pathways. Whilst drugs decisions will continue to be dynamic this is a remarkable proportion and a robust measure of normalisation. We have shown in both the pathways and journeys analyses that young people, by and large, make recognisable cost-benefit assessments and the fact that so many broadly settle primarily for cannabis rather than poly drug use is a clear illustration of this. It is important to distinguish at the extremes between the use of cannabis and the use of poly dance drugs in evaluating the scale of normalisation. Whilst many of our regular drug users have moved into combination drug repertoires and look set to continue for some years, as they transfer into the world of nightclubs where dance drug use is endemic (Release, 1997), they remain a discrete minority. Within the dance–nightclub world their behaviour is accepted and indeed celebrated but it is a moot point whether their actual drug taking, which is often judged excessive by more cautious peers, could be easily accommodated outside clubland. On the other hand the associated dance culture, the style, the music and actual dancing is widely embraced and ecstasy has filtered into more 'everyday' drug taking, for instance at informal parties. On balance our view is that the young adult dance drug scene of the late 1990s is part of the normalisation process, not in its origins but because it is now sustained by migration from the adolescent drugs pathways we have described (see Measham *et al.*, 1998).

We would want to review this assessment if, in particular, problem drug use becomes prevalent in this population and the dance drug scene becomes the readily identified source. In such circumstances the drugged-up, messed-up clubber might well become a symbol of excess, a techno junkie who has crossed the Rubicon beyond the recreational into the problematic and thus beyond wider peer accommodation.

Being drugwise

Although the notion of drugwise youth emerged from our surveys, particularly in the later years, the strongest sense that nearly all young people are drugwise comes from our interview data where abstainers demonstrated their considerable knowledge of the recreational drugs scene simply because they could not escape encounters with drugs and drug users. Whilst a 'soft' incidental measure of normalisation, it is nevertheless an important signal that abstainers have to negotiate and renegotiate their drugs status given that by simply being sociable, studying, training, working and going out at the weekends they regularly receive drug offers and observe drug use. Abstainers, former users and prospective triers were all able and willing to recount drugs stories based on drugs episodes involving siblings, friends, acquaintances and the local pub-club-party scene. Drugs are real to them; they no longer belong to an unknown subcultural world. One result of growing up drugwise was that with intellectual maturity and life experience most abstainers became pragmatic. They drew distinctions between gross misuse of 'hard drugs' on the one hand and 'sensible' recreational use of cannabis and to some extent amphetamines, LSD and ecstasy on the other. This moral accommodation of others' drug use based on a notion of freedom of choice as long as it did not harm anyone else is another essential dimension of the move towards normalisation. For abstainers, drug use remains 'deviant' but it is accommodated and rarely reported to officialdom. There is a growing 'matter of factness' about social drug use amongst contemporary youth. The most potent symbol of this is found in the way drug 'dealing', which carries serious sanctions under the law, is perceived by most young drug users as a sign of trust and friendship. 'Sorting' friends and acquaintances is rarely perceived as a serious criminal offence.

Future intentions

Traditionally, occasional drug trying in adolescence, particularly by well-adjusted young people, was interpreted as an example of 'normal' adolescent experimentation, rule testing and rebelliousness. No doubt these notions still have some explanatory power. However, as our pathways analysis showed, recreational drug use amongst our cohort and samples continues to escalate into young adulthood. The changes in pathways between 17 and 18 years of age were particularly salutary. With over a third of *former triers* returning to *in transition* and no less than 37 per cent of those previously *in transition* becoming *current drug users* in Year 5, we can see that prospective drug use or future intentions to try or reuse particular drugs remain powerful. This open-mindedness about future drug use, often by young adults who went through their adolescence without taking illicit drugs, is a further dimension in our particular thesis of normalisation.

Cultural accommodation of the illicit

We have spent considerable time highlighting the fact that developmental 'personality' theories which insist drug use is a sign of abnormality are inappropriate explanatory vehicles. Within sociology and much criminology the other theory most commonly associated with explanations of drug use is subcultural theory. Again, however, because the drug trying we are attempting to explain has moved from being a small minority to majority activity subcultural theory struggles. Indeed normalisation, because it is about the accommodation of previously 'deviant' activities into mainstream cultural arrangements, sits uncomfortably with subcultural explorations (unless we regard it primarily as a process). In a drugs subculture we find that the purchase, preparation and use of drugs becomes a preoccupation, a central component in users' lives. The armies of young adult, unemployed 'new' heroin users of the 1980s found that because of its physically addictive 'moreish' properties and high price, heroin use soon pulled them into lifestyles which centred on obtaining funds to continue their habit (Pearson *et al.*, 1986; Parker *et al.*, 1988). We find similar subcultural worlds revolving around crack cocaine use at the end of the 1990s (Parker *et al.*, 1998a) and it seems increasingly likely that we will enter the next millenium with regular heroin and combination drug use again becoming prevalent amongst socially excluded youth (Parker *et al.*, 1998b).

The drug use we have been describing in this study is quite different. It is largely recreational and is centred on less physically addictive drugs. It can be accommodated because most adolescents and young adult users merely fit their leisure into busy lives and then in turn fit their drug use into their leisure and 'time out' to compete alongside sport, holidays, romance, shopping, nights out, drinking and, most important of all, having a laugh with friends. Moreover as we have seen, such use now belongs as much with females as males and to young people from all social backgrounds.

If anything, the 1950s to 1980s characterised 'subcultural' drug use whilst the 1990s has seen the normalisation of a very different type of 'recreational' drug use. British youth culture has accommodated and perhaps facilitated recreational drug use both in terms of what is acceptable for young people to do and in absorbing and accommodating the language and imagery of drugs via the fashion, media, music and drink industries which thrive on youth markets (Parker *et al.*, 1995). The blurring of the licit and the illicit is an important aspect of normalisation. The close relationship, and pick-and-mix approach to drinking alcohol and recreational drug use we have identified is a salient example.

These then are the six dimensions of our normalisation thesis. Because the process is incomplete, because the epidemiological drama continues to unfold, we cannot be certain that the current trends will continue much further. Even if trying and use rates plateau, we will continue to move towards normalisation in the short term because such powerful social processes, like the proverbial oil tanker, simply do not suddenly change direction or come to a halt. Epidemiological trends once set as firmly as these nearly always have long lives.

Risk taking as a life skill

In Chapter 1 although we side-stepped entanglement with the theoretical debate about modernity be it 'post', 'late' or 'high', we outlined the universally agreed implications of growing up in modern times. The transition from childhood through adolescence on towards adulthood and full citizenship is now a longer, more uncertain journey. Whether we call this period between childhood and adulthood 'youth' or adolescence and post-adolescence is unimportant. What we are defining is a far longer period of semi dependency as young people spend more time in education and training, live at home longer, delay marriage and parenting and so on. Whilst objectively the levels of risk of 'failure' are still differentiated by race, gender, wealth, parental background, educational qualifications and neighbourhood, almost all young people *subjectively* experience this long period of uncertainty when they do not feel confident that the right opportunities, jobs and relationships will fall into place. The hardworking A-level student feels 'stressed out' just as much as the bored, under-trained, young shop assistant or indeed young offenders sitting in their cells for six months.

These subjective experiences, the feeling of negotiating in uncertainty, in a 'risk society', are the result of *individualisation* (Beck, 1992) whereby young people accept success or failure, prosperity or poverty as indicative of their own performance. Structural inequalities once emphasised by political and collective action and certain cultural understandings are no longer so loudly advocated as creating life chances by promoting or prohibiting success. Whether you get on is up to you (Roberts *et al.*, 1994). This type of conceptualising is clearly very different from the developmental and 'subcultural' approaches discussed earlier and indeed post-modernity theory in respect of youth culture reminds us that the processions of 'subcultural' youth formations of the post-war years are no longer so differentiated primarily because of the potency of social change in realigning and redefining class and inter-generational relationships (Furlong and Cartmel, 1997).

The normalisation of recreational drug use, we believe, is consistent with this type of theorising. There is a sense in all this that risk management has become routinised. Because the world owes you no favours and cannot tolerate indecision then perhaps taking no risks is simply too risky. You don't know if the education course, the training programme, the job offer will really deliver. You don't know if the shared flat or the cohabitation will work out, indeed there is evidence all around you that things may not. On the other hand, how else do you move on from the bedroom you've inhabited for eighteen years, get on and gain your privacy, your independence, the car, the clothes, the foreign holiday; not by winning the lottery, there's no risk of that. Put in this wider context, drugs decisions seem rather less dramatic. It is those adults unable to comprehend how much more complicated growing up has become who create the drama, as the moral panics documented in the first chapter illustrate.

This does not make drug taking safe or the drug user right. We have documented enough ill-conceived, drug using adventures and self-admissions of poor, often intoxicated, judgements to undermine such a conclusion. On the other hand rational decisions about consumption do lie at the heart of the normalisation thesis as they do with the McDonaldisation of modern societies. Our drug users are essentially extending the same decision-making processes to illicit drugs as others do in respect of cigarette smoking or drinking alcohol or indeed horse riding, hang gliding or mountaineering. It's your decision, you take the risks, you weigh the enjoyment and functional advantages to your life of your social habits against the potential dangers and pitfalls. Significantly the illegality of drug use and supplying is, as we have seen, rarely perceived as a key risk factor. This, interestingly, is despite the fact that in 1996 40,000 people were cautioned for cannabis possession in England and Wales compared with 4,000 in 1986. The rate of prosecution for possession has doubled to 24,000 over the same period and up to one thousand young people receive custodial sentences each year (*The Guardian*, 1998).

The connections between our longitudinal study of youth and drugs and this type of theoretical approach have emerged gradually and testing such an approach was certainly not an overt goal at the outset. In this sense we have used a 'grounded' strategy. Our respondents have spoken to us about the importance of leisure and friends and 'time out' as an antidote to struggles at school, college or in the employment market. They have recognised the need to be economical with the truth about their drug use when talking with adults. Parents' conceptions of risk and danger in respect of drugs are, to their mind, so misinformed and exaggerated that they regard lying as an act of concern for their elders' mental health. The cost-benefit risk assessment with which they decide how far to go to 'buzz' and get 'out of it' via alcohol or illicit drugs is an elaborate process. In reaching and reviewing their decisions, abstainers regularly conclude that drug users must make up their own minds. There is no more potent an expression of individualisation than their often-repeated conclusion that the poly drug users they know can be tolerated because 'its up to them if they want to kill themselves'. In the same way our drug triers and users, certainly once through early adolescence, vehemently refute peer pressure as a key factor in their decision to take drugs. Again they may not always be correct, but this is none the less their conclusion. It's how they believe they've got to where they are *vis à vis* drugs. They accept individual responsibility.

The followers of the regular drug user pathway, whilst critical of drugs education which is bland or moralistic or unable to mention the positive outcomes of drug use, also readily accept that risk and danger should be emphasised especially to warn off fair-weather experimenters. They are not denying risk nor are most viewing themselves as *invulnerable*. Their judgements may sometimes be poor but they appear to accept occasional bad experiences and negative outcomes as part and parcel of being a drug user. They accept their vulnerability though perhaps deny their mortality.

Rethinking the war on drugs

The misconceptions

In the first chapter we outlined the 'war on drugs' discourse showing how it has adapted to different waves of drugs 'problems' from the first heroin epidemic, through ecstasy and raves to young people's drug use. We are now in a better position to highlight the misconceptions and misunderstandings built into this *political* strategy to fight drug 'abuse' in young people.

Firstly the 'war on drugs' discourse, as laid out in *Tackling Drugs Together* and reiterated with little revision by New Labour, sees a direct link between teenage drug trying and crime. Young drug takers, even users of cannabis it is argued, will quickly become addicted to or disinhibited by their drugs and become young offenders spiralling out of control into a life of drugs and crime. The way to support this argument is to show that persistent young offenders take drugs from an early age, usually beginning with cannabis. This can of course be demonstrated; it is usually true that the small minority of young people who become persistent offenders from early adolescence also use drugs (Graham and Bowling, 1995). In each generation we find a disordered and damaged minority who are delinquents in adolescence and who have a tendency to remain criminogenic into their thirties (Moffitt, 1993). However, we could also say that this group tended to drink alcohol excessively even before their drug use so should we 'blame' alcohol? They also tended to grow up in care, be excluded from school and run away a lot. They often need psychiatric help (Rutter and Smith, 1994). Their drinking, like their drug use, is associated with their disordered and delinquent careers but it does not cause their anti-social behaviour. Their lives would be little different with or without 'designer' drinks or illicit drugs.

We have tracked such young people in this study but again they are a very small minority in any representative normal population. They are the exceptions and for this reason, whilst we need a specific strategy to deal with their problems and those they cause, we should not build an overall approach around them. For most young people recreational drug use, whilst itself illegal, is funded from the legitimate means of pocket money and part-time earnings. Moreover, as we have shown, our sample, including the drug users, mostly have either no or very light delinquent antecedents.

The second misconception is linked to the first but emphasises the addiction rather than crime spiral. However, there are very few signs of dependency in this recreational scene. Obviously we can find examples of this relationship and of course if we interview heroin or crack cocaine users they routinely display early poly drug use in their antecedents (Parker and Bottomley, 1996). However, much like our 'damaged' persistent delinquents, this pathway to problem drug use is rarely taken and again we find that most who take it have atypical social or psychological characteristics and vulnerabilities, many of which they share with the minority of drinkers who become alcoholics.

The next misconception which is widely held is that young people are pressured into drug use. Once again there are fragments of truth here and we too have found cases where, on reflection, older adolescents look back on initiations where they felt pressured. But again this is not usually the case. Our samples have insisted that they have made their own drugs decisions for which they take responsibility. They acknowledge peer influence but cite many other reasons such as curiosity, the need to relax, and most of all, rational hedonism. Not only is the notion of peer pressure as the central component of drug trying misconceived but it is a source of resentment to many young people when expounded by adults delivering drugs education. Moreover, as we have argued, because adolescents are social, peer-focused beings almost everything they do can be located in peer effects. This gets us nowhere.

The prevention side of the 'war on drugs' industry has developed a number of engaging arguments to defend and succour their position. Faced with the argument that, despite their expensive efforts – well in excess of £1.4 billion (White Paper 1998) to attempt to prevent young Britons taking drugs – adolescent drug use continues to climb, and they sigh with exasperation. There is, they point out, a simple reason for this. So dreadful is the problem that the war must be waged with far more intensity. More money must be spent, more time dedicated to prevention, we must start with 5 year olds! There is, for them, no other explanation. The suggestion that evaluations of numerous programmes (Dorn and Murji, 1992) are not encouraging is thus ignored. Instead the warriors reel off the anecdotes: examples of the young person whose death was ecstasy related, the drug-crazed young delinquent who terrorised a neighbourhood and the young woman who said she took drugs because her boyfriend pressured her. All these examples could be true. Their atypicality is ignored, however, because to acknowledge this would be to admit the need to make ideological room for a rational debate. The most extreme of the warriors go further. Non-believers must be suspect. 'You're a legaliser then?', 'You think drugs are good then do you?', 'You allow your children to take drugs?', 'So you think drugs are safe?'

In short, the resistance to discussing the meaning of young people's drug use and considering how to manage it at a societal level is very strong. It stems from a deep and genuine fear of illicit drug use, a hedonism taboo and a misunderstanding of the distinctions between drugs and types of use. Whilst we have noted signs of the gulf between parents and young people narrowing at a familial level and amongst many of those who work directly with young people, this process has not yet occurred in the highly politicised public policy debate.

Inconsistent regulation

Because young people's drug use seems unlikely to be a mere fashion or fad and because it has become entangled in the wider moral panic about and blaming of youth described in the first chapter then the last plank of normalisation, a truce between adults and youth about drugs, remains unlaid. Our own view is that strategic pragmatism will prevail, but not for several years yet. Whilst no one knows exactly how the UK will go about managing the normalisation of recreational drug use we do know the shortcomings and dysfunctions of current 'policy' which we should expect any new strategy to address and alleviate.

The ineffective use of resources on primary prevention is minor compared with the resources spent on enforcement. The processing of young people for cannabis possession dominates the policing contact with normalisation as it does all cautioning and prosecuting under the Misuse of Drugs Act. One of the unfortunate consequences of this is  that each of the forty-three police forces in England and Wales adopt slightly different official and unofficial responses. What happens to a young person found with cannabis is determined more by where he or she is processed than by what he or she has done. Formal responses vary from an on-the-spot warning to an informal caution, to a formal citable caution, to prosecution. Even more worryingly, whilst official policies vary, informal practices are also inconsistent. It is quite acceptable, 'unofficially', for officers simply to drop the offending drug down the drain and finger wag in some police areas, whereas this practice is genuinely discouraged in others. These inconsistencies are perpetrated through the courts. This differential distribution of justice can block educational, occupational and career routes or lead to dismissal in some jobs. 'Enforcement' at school or college is equally a lottery with well over a thousand young people being excluded for drugs incidents from English schools alone each year. These responses not only blight a young person's 'reputation' but make reintegration into the education system very difficult. Moreover being left at home and 'hanging out' for many months instead of being at school may not be the best way of preventing escalation of drug use if that is a probability in a particular young person. The Home Secretary's son, William Straw, might wish to count himself very lucky that his school took no action against him for supplying cannabis (*Sunday Times*, 28 December 1997).

These diverse and punitive responses are, as we have shown, much talked about by young people through drugs stories. Whilst for abstainers and the cautious ones they may act as a deterrent, they also reinforce the sense of unease with which young people view adult responses to them. Our interviewees often quoted the randomness and inconsistency of official responses as a symptom of the confusion and hypocrisy adults demonstrate in their reactions, particularly to cannabis. The moral authority of 'the law' was seen as badly undermined. This does little to facilitate citizenship and much to further disenchant young people in respect of politics, policing and public services.

The neglect of the public health dimension

The 'war on drugs' approach, because it has difficulty accepting that young people choose to take certain drugs and because it often pathologises those who do, has great difficulty dealing with reducing the harm or risks associated with drug use. To address these issues seriously involves accepting that drug use occurs and treating the user as a citizen – both of which grate with the most committed warriors. We see the hegemony of their approach when we consider how those very risks, dangers and worries, which our young drug users have raised, could be reduced by official intervention.

Again 'on the ground' we have a growing number of examples of harm-reduction practices but these are barely sanctioned in government strategy. Ideally this situation would be rectified through a holistic strategy supported by legislation and guidance through 'good practice' instructions. Here we merely give a handful of examples of how the public health imperative is being jeopardised by the 'unreal' drugs debate which dominates public and government thinking.

Currently, street drugs are quality unassured. They are not tested or regulated or codified in any official way. Drug dealers at the local level, the 'friends of friends' chain and the users have no idea what they are selling, buying or simply sharing. At present it is only the rules of encounter in the illegal market which maintain quality. We have heard many of our young subjects complain about badly cut amphetamines and unpredictable LSD doses. Many of the bad experiences and acute incidents have been put down to poor quality drugs. We know that a proportion of drugs-related deaths are linked to impurities or indeed exceptional and unexpected purity in the cases of heroin users. There are very few substances consumed by the public which are not regulated and inspected and yet young Britons ingest tens of millions of 'doses' of illicit drugs each week. It is estimated, for instance, that a million ecstasy-like tablets are consumed each week in the UK (Parliamentary Office of Science and Technology, 1996).

We have shown how through the sharing of information and experiences and recounting of 'drugs stories' young people try to reduce the risks of bad or very bad experiences from drugs adventures. There are undoubtedly harm reduction messages available, usually through voluntary street agency 'flyers', to help guide young users. However, this information is hard to come by and is generally not delivered to school-aged adolescents even in a targeted way, for instance, to those dance drug users who even at 16 are attending night clubs and dance clubs. The mixing of alcohol and drugs, particularly on weekend nights out, was at the source of many bad experiences and worrying incidents recounted during this study. Here is a harm reduction message demanding broadcast yet one which cannot be easily sent because of political sensibilities and the Establishment's need to keep alcohol and drugs in separate compartments.

Similarly because of the generation gulf and distrust of adult reactions noted in the earlier chapters, young drug users were reluctant to disclose their drug use to relatives or the family doctor even when they felt their drug taking might be causing or triggering ill health. This is an extremely worrying outcome both for young people and health professionals who are likely to misdiagnose and thus inappropriately treat their patients.

A further and related feature of official neglect of the public health imperative concerns the scientific knowledge deficit about the middle term and long term health effects of regular sustained dance drugs–poly drug use. We know that toxicity and neurotoxicity are increased by dose and regularity of use and that multiple drug ingestion tends to increase toxicity over and above the sum of the individual drugs (Parliamentary Office of Science and Technology, 1996). What we do not know is whether today's adolescent and young adult drug users are slowly damaging their health. We are unclear whether or not in ten or twenty years' time they will be susceptible to physical or more likely mental health problems perhaps related to seretonin transmitter damage in the brain.

Finally, the public health dimension embraces the wider population. Whilst driving after drinking alcohol is an activity associated with middle-aged and older Britons rather than youth, today's young Britons are far less fastidious about drug driving. The need to recognise this emerging problem and take responsibility for its management is yet another example of a failure to protect the public.

There is little doubt that the 'war on drugs' approach of consecutive Conservative administrations has been responsible for the neglect of the public health dimension. In firstly 'wasting' the early 1990s through neglect and then developing the *Tackling Drugs Together* approach with all its misconceptions, government has been unable to embrace and face the scale of normalisation and in turn has failed to recognise the need to manage and regulate the public health implications. This contrasts with the multiplicity of public health initiatives sanctioned when the injecting drug user–HIV connection was made in the mid 1980s. The strategic pragmatism shown then led to major health gains in respect of reducing needle sharing, unsafe sex and the spread of the HIV/AIDS virus. The difference of course was that it was also the health of non-drug users which was at stake. The 'just desserts' approach – drug users deserve all the problems they endure – had to be temporarily subverted.

Waiting for the truce

We are, unfortunately, some way away from the political moment when the dysfunctions of the 'war on drugs' strategy can be addressed. The important public policy issues – about how we deal with otherwise law abiding young citizens caught with drugs in their possession, and about how we ensure the health and safety of young people who use drugs – remain unresolved. This is because the complexities of drug use in the 1990s are obscured by ideological and political dogma and most of all by a lack of empathy for young people trying to grow up in modern times. We must wait for a truce before we can face up to the truth.

Bibliography

ACPO (1988) *Public Disorder Outside Metropolitan Areas*, London: Association of Chief Police Officers.

AIESEC/IPSOS (1993) *Generation 1993: A Study of the Views and Opinions of European Students*.

Aitken, P.P. (1978) *Ten-to-Fourteen Year Olds and Alcohol*, Edinburgh: HMSO.

Aldridge, J. and Measham, F. (submitted) 'Methodological issues surrounding the measurement of self-reported drinking frequency with youthful respondents'.

Aldridge, J., Measham, F. and Parker, H. (1996) *Drugs Pathways in the 1990s: Adolescents' Decision Making About Illicit Drug Use*, London: Drugs Prevention Initiative, Home Office.

Aldridge, J., Parker, H. and Measham, F. (1998) *Illicit Drug Trying and Use Across Adolescence* (working title), London: Drugs Prevention Initiative, Home Office.

Anderson, R., Kinsey, R., Loader, I. and Smith, C. (1991) *'Cautionary Tales': A Study of Young People and Crime in Edinburgh*, Edinburgh: Centre for Criminology, Edinburgh University.

Bagnall, G. (1988) 'Use of alcohol, tobacco and illicit drugs amongst 13-year-olds in three areas of Britain', *Drug and Alcohol Dependence* 22, pp. 242–251.

Balding, J. (1997) *Young People in 1996*, Schools Health Education Unit, University of Exeter.

Balding, J. and Regis, J. (1996) 'More alcohol down fewer throats', *Education and Health* 13, 4, pp. 61–64.

Barber, A., Corkery, J., and Ogunjuyigbe, K. (1996) *Statistics of Drugs Seizures and Offenders Dealt With, United Kingdom 1995*, Home Office Statistical Bulletin, 25/96.

Barnard, M., Forsyth, A. and McKeganey, N. (1996) 'Levels of drug use among a sample of Scottish school children', *Drugs: Education, Prevention and Policy*, 3 1, pp. 81–90.

Beck, U. (1992) *Risk Society: Towards a New Modernity*, London: Sage.

Becker, H. (1963) *Outsiders: Studies in the Sociology of Deviance*, New York: Free Press.

Brain, K. and Parker, H. (1997) *Drinking with Design: Alcopops, Designer Drinks and Youth Culture*, London: The Portman Group.

Brake, M. (1980) *The Sociology of Youth Culture and Youth Subcultures*, London: RKP.

Cairns, R. and Cairns, B. (1994) *Lifelines and Risk: Pathways of Youth in our Time*, New York: Harvester Wheatshead.

Campbell, A. (1981) *Girl Delinquents*, Oxford: Blackwell.

Carlen, P. (1996) *Jigsaw – A Political Criminology of Youth Homelessness*, Buckingham: Open University Press.

Cashmore, E. and Troyna, B. (1982) (eds) *Black Youth in Crisis*, London: Allen and Unwin.

Chisholm, L. and Bergeret, J.M. (1991) *Young People in the European Community. Towards an Agenda for Research and Policy*, Report to the Commission of the European Communities, Task Force, Education, Training and Youth, Brussels.

Chisholm, L. and Hurrelman, K. (1995) 'Adolescence in modern Europe: pluralised transition patterns and their implications for personal and social risks', *Journal of Adolescence* 18, pp. 129–158.

Coffield, F., Borril, C. and Marshall, S. (1986) *Growing Up At the Margins*, Milton Keynes: Open University Press.

Coffield, F. and Gofton, L. (1994) *Drugs and Young People*, London: Institute for Public Policy Research.

Cohen, S. (1973) *Folk Devils and Moral Panics*, London: Paladin.

Coleman, J. and Hendry, L. (1990) *The Nature of Adolescence*, London: Routledge.

Collin, M. (1997) *Altered State: The Story of Ecstasy Culture and Acid House*, London: Serpent's Tail.

Collins, L., Graham, J., Hansen, W. and Johnson, C. (1985) 'Agreement between retrospective accounts of substance use and earlier reported substance use', *Applied Psychological Measurement* 9, 3, pp. 301–309.

Collison, M. (1996) 'In search of the high life: drugs, crime, masculinity and consumption', *British Journal of Criminology* 36, 3, pp. 428–444.

Cooke, C., Macdonald, S. and Jones, I. (1997) 'Alcohol, tobacco and other drug use amongst secondary school children in Fife, Scotland', *Drugs: Education, Prevention and Policy* 4, 3, pp. 243–254.

Corrigan, P. (1979) *Schooling the Smash or Street Kids*, London: Macmillan.

Craig, J. (1997) *Almost Adult*, NISRA, Occasional Paper 3, Belfast.

Davies, A. (1992) *Leisure, Gender and Poverty: Working-Class Culture in Salford and Manchester, 1900–1939*, Buckingham: Open University Press.

Davies, J. and Farquahar, D. (1995) *Risk and Protective Factors Associated with Adolescent Drug Use*, Glasgow: University of Strathclyde.

Department of Health (1994) *Across the Divide*, London.

Dorn, N. and Murji, K. (1992) *Drug Preventions: A Review of the English Language Literature*, London: Institute for the Study of Drug Dependence.

Duffy, J. (1991) *Trends in Alcohol Consumption Patterns 1978–1989*, Oxon: NTC.

Evans, K. and Furlong, A. (1996) 'Metaphors of youth transition: niches, pathways, trajectories or navigations', seminar paper, Economic and Research Council, Swindon.

Fillmore, K. (1988) *Alcohol Use Across the Life Course*, Toronto: Addiction Research Foundation.

Fornäs, J. and Bolin, G (1995) *Youth Culture in Late Modernity*, London: Sage.

Forsyth, A. (1995) 'Ecstasy and illegal drug design: a new concept in drug use', *International Journal on Drug Policy* 6, 3, pp. 193–209.

Fossey, E. (1992) *Personal Communication* (quoted in Plant and Plant, 1992).

Furlong, A. and Cartmel, F. (1997) *Young People and Social Change*, Buckingham: Open University Press.

Gelder, K. and Thornton, S. (1997) *The Subcultures Reader*, London: Routledge.

Giddens, A. (1991) *Modernity and Self Identity*, Oxford: Polity.

Goddard, E. (1991) *Drinking in England and Wales in the Late 1980s*, London: HMSO.

Goddard, E. and Ikin, E. (1988) *Drinking in England and Wales in 1987*, London: HMSO.

—— (1996) *Teenage Drinking in 1994*, London: OPCS.

Gofton, L. (1990) 'On the town: drink and the new lawlessness', *Youth and Society* 29, pp. 33–39.

Goode, E. and Ben-Yehuda N. (1996) *Moral Panics: The Social Construction of Deviance*, Oxford: Blackwell.

Graeff, R. (1992) *Living Dangerously: Young Offenders in Their Own Words*, London: Harper Collins.

Graham, J. and Bowling, B. (1995) *Young People and Crime*, Home Office Research Study 145, London: Home Office.

The Guardian, 29 January 1998, 'Leap in numbers cautioned for having cannabis' (based on Commons written reply to Paul Flynn, MP)

Hagell, A. and Newburn, T. (1996) 'Family and social contexts of adolescent re-offenders', *Journal of Adolescence* 19, 1, pp. 5–18.

Hall, S. and Jefferson, T. (1976) (eds) *Resistance through Rituals*, London: Hutchinson.

Hammersley, R. (1994) *Use of Controlled Drugs in Scotland: data from the 1993 Scottish Crime Survey*, Central Research Unit, The Scottish Office.

Hammersley, R., Ditton, J. and Main, D. (1997) 'Drug use and sources of drug information in a 12–16-year-old school sample', *Drugs: Education, Prevention and Policy* 4, 3, pp. 231–241.

Harrison, B. (1971) *Drink and the Victorians*, London: Faber and Faber.

Hawker, A. (1978) *Adolescents and Alcohol*, London: Edsall.

Hawkins, J., Catalare, R. and Miller, J. (1992) 'Risk and protective factors for alcohol and other drugs problems in adolescence and early adulthood' *Psychological Bulletin* 112, 1, pp. 64–105.

Health Education Authority (1996) *Drug Realities*, London.
—— (1996) *Young People and Alcohol*, London.
Hebdige, D. (1979) *Subculture: The Meaning of Style*, London: Methuen.
Heidensohn, F. (1985) *Women and Crime*, London: Macmillan.
Henderson, S. (1997) *Ecstasy: Case Unsolved*, London: Pandora.
HMSO (1994) *Tackling Drugs Together*, London.
Hollands, R. (1995) *Friday Night, Saturday Night: Youth Cultural Identification and the Post-industrial City*, Newcastle: University of Newcastle upon Tyne.
Hough, M. and Roberts, J. (1998) *Attitudes to Punishment: 1996 British Crime Survey*, London: Home Office.
Hughes, K., MacKintosh, A.M., Hastings, G., Wheeler, C., Watson, J. and Inglis, J. (1997) 'Young people, alcohol and designer drinks: quantitative and qualitative study', *British Medical Journal*, 314.
Irwin, S. (1995) 'Social reproductional change in the transition from youth to adulthood', *Sociology* 29, pp. 293–315.
ISDD (1994) *Drug Misuse in Britain 1993*, London: Institute for the Study of Drug Dependence.
—— (1996) *Drug Misuse in Britain 1995*, London: Institute for the Study of Drug Dependence.
Jahoda, G. and Cramond, J. (1972) *Children with Alcohol: A Developmental Study in Glasgow*, London: HMSO.
James, W.H., Kim, G.K. and Moore, D.D. (1997) 'Examining racial and ethnic differences in Asian adolescent drug use: the contributions of culture, background and lifestyle', *Drugs: Education, Prevention and Policy* 4, 1, pp. 39–51.
Jones, G. (1991) 'From dependency to citizenship? Transitions to adulthood in Britain', Paper presented to workshop on Longitudinal Strategy in the Study of Youth, Moscow Youth Institute.
Leitner, M., Shapland, J., and Wiles, P. (1993) *Drug Usage and Prevention*, London: Home Office.
Lemmens, P. (1994) 'The alcohol content of self-report and "standard" drinks', *Addiction* 89, pp. 593–601.
McKeganey, N., Forsyth, A., Barnard, M., and Hay, G. (1996) 'Designer drinks and drunkenness amongst a sample of Scottish school children', *British Medical Journal* 313, 17 August, p. 401.
McKeganey, N. (1997) *Pre-teen Drug Users in Scotland*, University of Glasgow.
McNeish, D. (1996) 'Young people, crime, justice and punishment' in Roberts and Sachdiv, 1996: 77–98.
Maffesoli, M. (1995) *The Time of the Tribes*, Aldershot: Sage.
Marsh, A., Dobbs, J. and White, A. (1986) *Adolescent Drinking*, London: HMSO.
Marsh, P. and Fox Kibby, K. (1992) *Drinking and Public Disorder*, London: Portman.

Marsh, P., Rosser, E. and Harré, R. (1978) *The Rules of Disorder*, London: Routledge and Kegan Paul.

May, C. (1992) 'A burning issue? Adolescent alcohol use in Britain', *Alcohol and Alcoholism* 27, 2, pp. 109–115.

Measham, F. (1996) 'The "Big Bang" approach to sessional drinking: Changing patterns of alcohol consumption amongst young people in north west England', *Addiction Research*, 4, 3, pp. 282–299.

Measham, F., Aldridge, J. and Parker, H. (1998) 'The teenage transition: from recreational drug use to the dance drug culture', *Journal of Drug Issues*, Special Edition, 28, 1, pp. 9–22.

Meikle, A., McCallum, C., Marshall, A. and Coster, G. (1996) *Drugs Survey on a Selection of Secondary School Pupils in the Glasgow Area Aged 13–16*, Glasgow Drugs Prevention Team, Glasgow.

Miller, W., Heather, N. and Hall, W. (1991) 'Calculating standard drink units: international comparisons', *British Journal of Addiction*, 86, pp. 43–47.

Miller, P. and Plant, M. (1996) 'Drinking, smoking and illicit drug use among 15 and 16-year-olds in the United Kingdom', *British Medical Journal* 313, pp. 394–7.

Moffit, T. (1993) 'Adolescence – limited and lifecourse persistent anti-social behaviour: a developmental taxonomy', *Psychological Review* 100, 4, pp. 674–701.

Moores, S. (1993) *Interpreting Audiences: The Ethnography of Media Consumption*, Aldershot: Sage.

Mott, J. (1992) (ed.) *Crack and Cocaine in England*, London: Home Office RPU Paper 70.

Mukhtar, T. (1997) *Persistent Young Offenders/Persistent Young Consumers*, Report to the Thames Valley Partnership.

Muncie, J. (1984) *The Trouble with Kids Today: Youth and Crime in Post War Britain*, London: Hutchinson.

Mungham, G. and Pearson, G. (1976) (eds) *Working Class Youth Culture*, London: Routledge and Kegan Paul.

Newburn, T. and Hagell, A. (1994) *Persistent Young Offenders*, London, Policy Studies Institute.

Newcombe, R., Measham, F. and Parker, H. (1994) 'A survey of drinking and deviant behaviour among 14/15 year olds in north-west England', *Addiction Research* 2, 4, pp. 319–341.

Oakley, A. (1996) 'Gender matters: man the hunter' in Roberts and Sachdiv, 1996: 23–41.

Oakley, A., Branned, J. and Dodd, K. (1992) 'Young people, gender and smoking in the UK', *Health Promotion International* 7, pp. 75–88.

Otero-Lopez, J., Luengo-Martin, A., Miron-Redendo, L., Carrillo-de-la Peña, M., and Romero-Triñanes, E. (1994) 'An empirical study of the relations between drug abuse and delinquency amongst adolescents', *British Journal of Criminology* 34, 4, pp. 459–478.

Parker, H. (1974) *View from the Boys*, Newton Abbott: David and Charles, republished Gregg Revivals, 1992.
—— (1996) 'Alcohol, young adult offenders and criminological cul de sacs', *British Journal of Criminology* 36, 2.
—— (1997) *Managing the Normalisation of Recreational Drug Use Amongst Young Britons*, Association of Chief Police Officers Drugs Conference, Leicestershire.
Parker, H. and Bottomley, T. (1996) *Crack Cocaine and Drugs Crime Careers*, London: Home Office Publications Unit.
Parker, H. and Measham, F. (1994) 'Pick 'n' mix: changing patterns of illicit drug use amongst 1990s adolescents', *Drugs: Education, Prevention and Policy* 1, 1, pp. 5–13.
Parker, H., Newcombe, R. and Bakx, K. (1988) *Living with Heroin: The Impact of a Drugs Epidemic on an English Community*, Milton Keynes: Open University Press.
Parker, H., Measham, F. and Aldridge, J. (1995) *Drugs Futures: Changing Patterns of Drug Use Amongst English Youth*, London: Institute for Study of Drug Dependence (reprinted 1996).
Parker, H., Brain, K. and Bottomley, T. (1998a) *Evolving Crack Cocaine Careers: New Users, Quitters and Long Term Combination Drug Users in N.W. England*, Home Office Research and Statistics Directorate.
Parker, H., Egginton, R. and Bury, C. (1998b) *New Heroin Outbreaks Amongst Young People in England and Wales at the end of the 1990s*, London: Report to the Police Research Group, Home Office.
Parliamentary Office of Science and Technology (1996) *Common Illegal Drugs and Their Effects: Cannabis, ecstasy, amphetamines and LSD*, London: POST.
Patrick, J. (1973) *A Glasgow Gang Observed*, London: Eyre Methuen.
Pearson, G. (1983) *Hooligan: A History of Respectable Fears*, London: Macmillan.
Pearson, G., Gilman, M. and McIver, S. (1986) *Young People and Heroin: An Examination of Heroin Use in the North of England*, London: Health Education Council.
Perry, 6., Jupp, B., Perry, H. and Laskey, K. (1997) *The Substance of Youth*, York: Joseph Rowntree Foundation.
Petridis, A. (1996) 'How much ecstasy do the British really take?', *Mixmag* 2, 62, July, pp. 98–100.
Plant, M. (1975) *Drugtakers in an English Town*, London: Tavistock.
Plant, M. and Plant, M. (1992) *Risk-Takers: Alcohol, Drugs, Sex and Youth*, London: Tavistock/Routledge.
Plant, M., Peck, D. and Samuel, E. (1985) *Alcohol, Drugs and School Leavers*, London: Tavistock/Routledge.
Plant, M., Bagnall, G., Foster, J. and Sales, J. (1990) 'Young people and drinking: results of an English national survey', *Alcohol and Alcoholism* 25, 6, 685–690.

Power, R., Power, T. and Gibson, N. (1996) 'Attitudes and experience of drug use amongst a group of London teenagers', *Drugs: Education, Prevention and Policy* 3, 1, pp. 71–80.

Pryce, K. (1979) *Endless Pressure*, Harmondsworth: Penguin.

Ramsay, M. and Spiller, J. (1997) *Drug Misuse Declared in 1996: Latest Results from the British Crime Survey*, Home Office Research Survey 172, London: Home Office.

Redhead, S. (1993) *Rave Off*, Aversbury: Aldershot.

Release (1997) *Release Drugs and Dance Survey*, London: Release.

Roberts, K., Clark, S. and Wallace, C. (1994) 'Flexibility and individualisation: a comparison of transitions into employment in England and Germany', *Sociology* 28, 1, pp. 31–54.

Roberts, C., Moore, L., Blakey, V., Playle, R. and Tudor-Smith, C. (1995) 'Drug use among 15–16-year-olds in Wales 1990–94', *Drugs: Education, Prevention and Policy* 2, 3, pp. 305–317.

Roberts, H. and Sachdev, D. (1996) (eds) *Young People's Social Attitudes: The Views of 12–19-Year-Olds*, Ilford: Barnardos.

Roberts, C., Kingdon, A., Frith, C., and Tudor-Smith, C. (1997) *Young People in Wales: Lifestyle Changes 1986–96*, Cardiff: Health Promotion Wales.

Rowlands, O., Singleton, N., Maher, J. and Higgins, V. (1997) *Living in Britain: Results from the 1995 General Household Survey*, London: Office for National Statistics Social Survey Division.

Royal College of Psychiatrists (1986) *Alcohol our Favourite Drug*, London: Tavistock.

Rutter, M. (1989) 'Pathways from childhood to adult life', *Journal of Child Psychology and Psychiatry* 30, 1, pp. 23–51.

Rutter, M. and Smith, D. (1994) (eds) *Psycho-social Disorders in Young People*, Chichester: John Wiley.

Ryan, P. (1991) *International Comparisons of Vocational Education and Training for Intermediate Skills*, London: Falmer Press.

Saunders, N. (1995) *Ecstasy and the Dance Culture*, London: Nicholas Saunders.

Saunders, N. (1997) *Ecstasy Reconsidered*, London: Nicholas Saunders.

Scottish Council on Alcohol (1996) 'Young people and alcohol in Scotland: a survey of branded preferences of 15–17-year-olds', Glasgow.

Shiner, M. and Newburn, T. (1996) *The Youth Awareness Programme: An Evaluation of a Peer Education Drugs Project*, London, Drugs Prevention Initiative, Home Office.

Smith, C. and Nutbeam, D. (1992) 'Adolescent drug use in Wales', *British Journal of Addiction* 87, pp. 227–233.

Smith, R. (1997) *Implications of the Criminal Justice and Public Order Act for Youth Culture in the Suburban South East*, Final Report to ESRC, Swindon.

Southern Health and Social Services Board (1993) 'Illicit drug and solvent use', in ISDD (1994) *Drug Misuse in Britain: Annual Audit of Statistics 1994*, London: Institute for the Study of Drug Dependence.

Stares, P. (1996) *Global Habit: The Drug Problem in a Borderless World*, Washington: Brookings Institute.

Sumner, C. (1994) *The Sociology of Deviance: An Obituary*, Buckingham: Open University Press.

Taylor, I., Walton, P. and Young, J. (1973) *The New Criminology*, London: RKP.

Thornton, S. (1995) *Club Cultures: Music, Media and Subcultural Capital*, Cambridge: Polity Press.

Tuck, M. (1989) *Drinking and Disorder: A Study of Non-Metropolitan Violence*, HORPU Research Report 108, London: HMSO.

Turner, C. (1990) 'How much alcohol is in a "standard drink"? An analysis of 125 studies', *British Journal of Addiction* 85, 1,171–1,175.

Webb, E., Ashton, C., Kelly, P., and Kamali, F. (1996) 'Alcohol and drug use in UK university students', *Lancet* 348, pp. 922–5.

White Paper (1998) *Tackling Drugs to Build a Better Britain*, Cmnd. 3945, London: Stationary Office.

Wibberley, C. (1997) 'Young people's feelings about drugs', *Drugs: Education, Prevention and Policy* 4, 1, pp. 65–79.

Wilkins, L. (1964) *Social Deviance*, London: Tavistock.

Wilkinson, C. (1995) *The Drop Out Society*, Leicester: National Youth Agency.

Willis, P. (1977) *Learning to Labour*, London: Saxon House.

Wolfensberger, W. (1972) *Normalisation*, Toronto: Institute for Mental Retardation.

Wright, J. and Pearl, L. (1990) 'Knowledge and experience of young people regarding drug abuse 1969–1989', *British Medical Journal* 300, pp. 99–103.

Young, J. (1971) *The Drug Takers*, London: Paladin.

Index

t denotes table. f denotes figure.